EXPLORING THE WONDERL

INDIAN
WORK FORCE
38 CASE STUDY IDEAS IN HR & OB
WITH QUESTIONS AND SUGGESTED ANSWERS

DR. ASIM KUMAR BANDYOPADHYAY

BlueRose
Publishers
NewDelhi • London

Republished in December 2021
BLUEROSE PUBLISHERS
www.bluerosepublishers.com
info@bluerosepublishers.com
+91 8882 898 898

Distributed by: BlueRose, Amazon, Flipkart

DEDICATION

A humble tribute to my parents who are no more with me:

Any good thing I do, it is all because of you, your unconditional love, care and support. Regardless of whichever corner of this vast universe you two are eternally resting in, I always feel the warmth of your presence, it is so re-assuring.

I tearfully recollect those days of my childhood, when, at times, our future looked so bleak, so threatening, so challenging and overwhelmingly hopeless. Everything used to seem lost. But your courage, strength of character, fortitude and forbearance saw us through those dark days and we could keep our feet firmly on the ground.

Years later, when I established myself in my professional life, at times, I got let down, cheated, bruised, battered, badly beaten, insulted and humiliated, I went back and took shelter in your arms. On every such occasion, you sheltered me, nourished me, consoled and encouraged me. I bounced back with renewed vigour.

The value system you inculcated in us, the siblings, in our childhood, still serve as beacons in advanced stages of our lives.

Even today, whenever I feel lonely and uncared for, I remember you and feel the comfort of your presence and nurturing. With a great sense of gratitude, I am dedicating this compilation, my first book, to the memory of both of you. I need your blessing throughout the rest of my life.

– Asim Bandyopadhyay

FOREWORD

Dr Asim Kumar Bandyopadhyay is a doyen of management education with empowering students with not just lessons of management but lessons of life. His quest for knowledge and understanding has endeared him with qualification from the best institutions in our Country. His wisdom is derived from the vast experience that he has garnered over 5 decades from industry as an employee, as an entrepreneur having set up his own firm in the domain of electronics, as an educationist and trainer among the best educational institutions.

I am extremely happy that Dr Asim Kumar Bandyopadhyay has come forward to share his experiences in the form of case studies primarily those relating to human resources and organisational behaviour. Academicians have always felt a need for more examples and cases pertaining to the Indian business scenario as most books were of foreign authors and gave examples of other country and rarely India. This book fills in that void and brings to the table an Indian perspective embedding in it the dimensions actually faced by the Indian corporate sector.

I am sure that the readers of this book will find it highly engaging and enriching in their pursuit of corporate or academic careers.

Dr. H. Muralidharan

Dean, Ramaiah Institute of Management, Bangalore

INTRODUCTION: WHY I HAVE WRITTEN THIS BOOK.

"Take my asset away, leave my people; in five years, I will have it all back."

– Alfred Sloan, General Motors

"Human resource is not a thing we do; it is the thing that runs our business."

– Steve Wynn, Wynn Las Vegas

Interestingly, for years and years of my industrial career, the role and importance of HRM were beyond me i.e. my understanding, comprehension and even my psyche, let alone any appreciation. I always managed to convince myself and believe that HRM was the simplest and least challenging of all the disciplines of management that I encountered. My reasoning was ridiculously simple. Assume you have a handful of grains, say boiled rice in your fist and you throw them around. How many birds, say crows and pigeons will surround you? Will there be any dearth of these flying creatures around you, each aspiring to have a mouthful of these grains? Or assume you have a piece of bread in your hand and you throw it on the road. How many street dogs will pounce on it?

Am I, by any chance, equating human resources with birds and animals? Definitely not; I am not out of my mind, at least as yet. I have great regard for human resources. All that I mean is, if you have the capacity and willingness to pay, you can, as well, hire the best of minds and retain them. It is only your capacity and willingness to pay that matter. Not much of management genius is required there; human resources are available and retainable. I had nurtured this idea for a good one and a half decades until I was rudely shocked by the turn of events which taught me otherwise around my mid-career when I was heading a department. There was, however, one more not so glorifying reason for me to underestimate HRM. I observed over the years that upper mid-level executives from technical/operational streams who reached their ultimate level of competence, i.e. no longer promotable, but had a good number of years of service left, were transferred to HRM (called Personnel Departments those days) or Purchase Departments and, lo and behold, they could get one or even two promotions before their retirement. Management policy and practice of that kind gave me an undue liberty to surmise that the Personnel and Purchase departments were safe heavens and the last resorts of incompetent and unworthy left over from the technical i.e. line departments.

Subsequently, I observed with wide eyed horror how the policy and practice of undermining HRM took its toll and cost the organizations in the corporate world dearly in course of time. Talented and gifted people were uncared for and left in droves only to cool their heels at home. Innocent and sincere executives who committed small mistakes inadvertently and unknowingly were victimized and disproportionately punished. Competent and dedicated people who displayed courage and initiative were singled out and harassed. Ultimately, the HRM departments, through their malfunctioning and repeated blunders confirmed the resounding dictum from the great Sermon on the Mount: "Blessed are the meek because they will inherit the earth."

One's own life experience is the biggest teacher in one's life. Experience has taught me the importance and significance of HRM and how it can make or break an organization. My professional exposure has been in technical and line areas and hence, my personal resources to compose a book on the theoretical aspects of HRM are inadequate. But today, as I have retired and taken shelter in academic pursuits to keep myself professionally engaged, away from the heat and dust of a manufacturing industry, I feel compelled to sit in one corner, recollect and pen down my experiences with the fond hope that sometimes, somewhere in any portion of this vast universe, someone may read these narrations and derive benefits of not repeating the managerial blunders chronicled here. If such a thing happens, I shall consider myself fortunate and be thankful to the almighty. This is my humble gift to the world of academics and the practising mangers alike.

To conclude, there are a few words of caution for the readers. The purpose of this book is not malice and tarnishing the image of any organization or individual is the last thing in my mind. The names and identities of the organizations and individuals mentioned in this book are imaginary and do not resemble any real life entity to the best of my knowledge. The purpose of writing this book is entirely academic and not intended to hurt anyone in real life. If there is any similarities with any real life entity, that would only be an unwanted coincidence and unintentional and should be viewed as such.

Dr. Asim Kumar Bandyopadhyay

(Adjunct Professor, Ramaiah Institute of Management, Bangalore)

Dated: 11th February, 2018.

DISCLAIMER

This compilation of case studies in Human Resources Management and Organizational Behaviour has resulted from several decades of professional experience of the author. This collection has been made only for teaching and training of students and trainees of management courses in management institutions and training establishments and also for enlightenment of the practitioners and professionals in HRM and OB areas.

This compilation is purely an academic exercise and should be considered as such. This exercise does not propose to or purport to hurt the sentiments of any individual, organization, community, religious groups, language groups or association of people nor it is intended to put any such entity into disrepute or bad light.

All the names of individuals, companies, organizations or institutions used and mentioned here are imaginary and fictional without any resemblance to any real life entity. If any such resemblance or similarity is found at a later date, it should be treated as a purely accidental, unintended and unwarranted coincidence.

– Asim Bandyopadhyay

CONTENTS

CASE STUDY 1

YEARNING FOR MARITAL BLISS AND PLUNGING ON TO MOTHER EARTH

Ambatti Suryaprakash Reddy, an alumnus of JNTU, Hyderabad, has been a seasoned Hyderabadi and a proud professional in his mid –twenties. He is tall and majestic and a keen sportsman acquiring prowess in basket ball and table tennis, the games in which he used to represent his University in inter University tournaments. A graduate in Computer Science, he, within himself desired to join the armed forces. Given his physique and personality, he could have, as well, made it provided, of course, he could appear at the SSB. Being the eldest of three siblings, the other two being sisters, he was the proverbial 'apple of his mother's eyes.' The only son of a school teacher, he was deeply patriotic and wanted to join the defense forces to serve his country. But, his fate dictated otherwise.

A small group of officers from the defense forces visited JNTU campus and held preliminary selection interviews for the outgoing graduates. Suryaprakash appeared and got selected and was called for the final selection at Jabalpur. But, when he was about to leave his home with a loaded suitcase in hand, to board the train to Jabalpur, there was a high drama enacted by his mother and sisters. The three were wailing inconsolably as if a great tragedy had already befallen. The demonstration of unexplained grief was led by his mother who firmly believed that joining the armed forces was tantamount to signing one's own death sentence, sooner or later he was going to die. Suryaprakash was flabbergasted, but could not ignore his mother. He reluctantly called it off.

But, God was benevolent to Suryaprakash and his family at least at that time. The next time, it was the turn of DCS, the biggest software service provider of the country to visit the campus and all the final semester computer science students got chance to appear and, of course, Suryaprakash made it with flying colours. The job involved nine to twelve month's extensive professional training in identified domain specific areas of business of interest of DCS clientele. Computer science graduates knew software not business, so for designing software to automate business areas, these trainings were needed. The glittering silver lining was that the training was to be conducted at Hyderabad itself so that Suryaprakash could attend the whole program staying with his parents. It was a virtual bonanza for the family, albeit short lived.

The training continued for full twelve months and Suryaprakash's heavenly salary was fully saved and it became a substantial amount so much so that his father became bold enough to look for a suitable match for his first daughter, elder of the two and next to Suryaprakash. In the meanwhile something more surprising was brewing up for the family. Suryaprakash got posted in distant California i.e. the west coast of USA on the pacific. So, He had to pack his bags again, not destined to one of India's border in kargil or Jaishalmer, but to one of DCS's client's premises in the west coast of the most powerful country of the world. This time, the ladies of the family celebrated by distributing sweets in the neighborhood instead.

Suryaprakash's life in the states was far from sweet and honey; he took a couple of years to get accustomed to the accent and food habits which he could eventually overcome. But he became desperately home sick because of work pressure and he could not get any leave to see his parents and sisters back in Hyderabad. But, soon there was good news from home and a sign of relief on the horizon. In one of the promising alliances his father was negotiating, there was an exchange proposal i.e. Suryaprakash and his sister had to get married to the daughter and son of that family respectively. The family was quite decent and their demand quite moderate. They had also seen his sister and liked her and it was now Suryaprakash's turn to visit Hyderabad to see their daughter.

He could barely manage to get a few days' leave, landed in Hyderabad and visited the family with his parents. The girl turned out to be sweet, beautiful and accomplished much to his liking. He was dumbstruck and smitten, gave his consent to the parents and rushed back to California only to arrange for the next span of leave within a gap of three months. But this time, God had something else designed for him. His employer could locate a very promising client in Brazil and transferred him there. He was required to undergo a crash course in Spanish and cross culture training as per the company's policy of posting expatriates in a non-English speaking country. He was also told, point blank, there was no question of getting any leave within the next one year or so. He was asked to pack up his bags immediately and proceed to Brazil.

Suryaprakash was devastated. Not only was his own, but his sister's marriage also in jeopardy. He did not proceed to Brazil; he went to the terrace of the huge office building overlooking the magnificent golden gate bridge on the San-Fransisco Bay and took a plunge on to the mother earth under the force of gravity. His mutilated body under a pool of blood was discovered by the security staff.

Questions:

i. Was there any problem with Suryaprakash's upbringing that could be held responsible for the tragedy, directly or indirectly?

From the narration of the case it may be concluded that his upbringing was, at least, indirectly responsible for the tragedy. His was a closely knit family based on deep affection and love, like many other Indian lower middle class families. He was too much attached to his family and though physically strong, he was mentally not strong enough to withstand the vicissitudes of a tough corporate life.

ii. Were his parents right on their part?

The issue is mainly between Suryaprakash and his employer. But, as we have discussed in the previous question, his upbringing had a bearing, albeit indirect, on his reaction to his employer's moves and actions. Once we consider upbringing, parents are implicated. The culture and atmosphere in the family were not simply conducive enough for

Suryaprakash to withstand the rough and tumble in a career in a highly profit motivated multinational private corporate sector.

iii. Was the employer right on their part?

Absolutely not. It was an Indian multinational and hence the management should have been fully aware of the Indian values and ethos when they employ Indians in India. The employer should have taken care of the following:

a. Be aware of family issues that may have serious bearing on the executive's professional engagement with the company.

b. Not to disregard but to respect the value systems, culture and outlook of a typical lower middle class, education based, family in India and their myriad socio-economic compulsions.

c. Be aware that the core competence of the company is derived from the contributions of a class of employees whose priorities and sensibilities should be understood and valued in the proper perspective.

iv. Was Suryaprakash right on his part?

Committing suicide being demoralized by this kind of provocation cannot be a right step. Without succumbing to the overwhelming but momentary disappointment, he should have realized what would be the implication of his extreme step on his sisters and parents. By this drastic action, all the stakeholders have lost; he lost his life, his parents and sisters a bread winner of the family and his employer, a bright and promising employee. Nobody has gained anything except, perhaps, the company might have learnt a few hard lessons.

v. What lesson you derive in HRM from this case study?

We should derive a few valuable lessons from this case:

a. When a knowledge employee like Suryaprakash comes to work for a company, he works for the welfare of himself and his family, the interest of the other stake holders may not be supreme in his mind. He should never be provoked to feel that his interests can be sacrificed for the sake of company's larger interests.

b. HR functions should be decentralized as much as practicable. Even in a centralized set up, there should be identified functionaries whom the engineers can turn to and confide even sometimes regarding their personal or family issues, they should never be allowed to feel left high and dry.

c. There is no alternative to counseling and grooming whenever an engineer is sent abroad on professional assignments.

d. There should always be proper arrangement for adequate leave and relief to attend to family exigencies as and when serious issues arise.

e. In the absence of the arrangements mentioned above, Suryaprakash's parents may move court for compensation; the company should be ready with adequate defense.

GHASTLY DOUBLE DEATH AND ITS AFTERMATH

Mr. Sridhar Murthy felt totally dispirited and dejected as he was sitting in his favourite easy chair, his father's legacy, in the living room of his modest flat in Basavangudi, central Bangalore. Even the din and bustle of D.V. Gundappa road below could not shake him up from his stupor. Just the day before i.e. yesterday, he was suspended from service, pending enquiry, being accused of grave professional negligence, carelessness, dereliction of duty, etc.

Of course, the matter was indeed very grave, Mr. Sridhar Murthy, during his twenty seven years of service in the industry had not seen such a tragedy before. It was just like a shocking drama. All that he can recollect now under his overwhelming mental distress is that, as an in-charge of the environmental chamber, he was in the 10 AM to 6 PM shift. It was unusual and odd shift timing for him, he was not accustomed with. One of his colleagues had to go on leave suddenly owing to some medical emergency in the family and Sridhar Murthy, who works normally in the 8 AM to 4 PM shift, was asked to replace him, at least, for the time being.

Human beings are slaves of habit, so they say. Sridhar Murthy was habituated to take a brief nap at around 5 PM after getting back home and at 5:30 PM he was used to sip a cup of hot filtered coffee made by his wife. But on that D-day, he was on duty during those hours and he felt sleepy as usual. He longed for a cup of coffee to ward off sleep and was about to get up from his chair for a walk up to the canteen. All of a sudden, the phone rang and the call was from the security office at the front gate. Two visitors had come and wanted to see the functioning of the environmental chamber. They were officials from a renowned private sector industry in Bangalore. They had obtained the necessary clearance from the top management to see the environmental testing facilities.

"5 PM is not the right time for a factory visit." – Sridhar Murthy was grumbling within himself. He had to put off his visit to the canteen for a while, albeit reluctantly. He sacrificed as long as fifteen minutes waiting for the visitors to arrive, but they did not show up, as if they got lost somewhere along the way. Sridhar Murthy felt impatient and walked out. But before leaving the chamber unguarded and unattended, he did not forget to turn back and check, the red warning light was on and the message was shining: "Caution-the chamber is ON." "The chamber was on means it was nitrogen fired" – he thought within himself while leaving.

He took about twenty minutes to go and come but was shell shocked to see the chamber door slightly open and nitrogen fumes leaking out when he returned. "Somebody had played a mischief." – He was trembling with fear and excitement. At that time his reliever arrived to take over but Murthy forgot about going home. He narrated to his colleague what all had happened. Both of them decided to switch off the chamber, switch on the fan and drain off the nitrogen opening the door fully. It took about half an hour to go inside to check what exactly had happened. The equipment under test was intact, but there were two more unwanted things: two human bodies, apparently unconscious, lying by the side of the equipment.

Though stupefied and stunned, the duo did not lose their brains, called the security that brought the stretcher to carry the bodies to the factory hospital without delay. The doctors on duty immediately checked the bodies and declared "Brought dead." During the same evening, news reached the top brass through security. Upon preliminary enquiry, it came to light that the two engineers, after collecting their security passes, were walking to Murthy's department. On the way, they met another acquaintance and stopped for about fifteen minutes for chatting while Murthy was waiting. The duo, due to some mysterious reason did not heed the warning and went inside the chamber in Murthy's absence. They died due to suffocation as the whole chamber was nitrogen fired. Murthy was summarily suspended pending detailed enquiry. The private company later sued Murthy's employer for a hefty compensation.

Questions:

i. Do you think Mr. Murthy was at fault longing for a cup of coffee at that time?

    The very fact that the canteen was open and coffee was available, indicate that the rules of the industry permitted drinking coffee at that time. Mr. Murthy, while leaving the chamber on, unattended and unguarded, should have informed the security of his intention to go for coffee. The security should have sensed the risk and could have sent a reliever for about fifteen/twenty minutes.

ii. Do you think Murthy can be blamed for dereliction of duty and he can be held responsible for the tragedy?

    Undeniably, there was dereliction of duty on Murthy's part as has been explained in the answer to the previous question. But, he can't be held solely responsible for the tragedy. The two visitors, who died, being technical persons, should not have ignored the warning under any circumstances. Nobody should enter a nitrogen fired environmental chamber without putting on oxygen masks. They should have waited for Murthy's arrival.

iii. Do you think Murthy's employer was right in allowing the visitor at that time?

    It appears from the narration of the case that proper indication of the time restriction was not conveyed to the visitors. Murthy should have been informed of the visit beforehand not by the security but by a higher officer. The security could come to know about the visit only when the two visitors arrived at the security gate. Moreover, the security should not have allowed the two visitors walk inside the factory without accompanying them.

iv. Do you think the visiting engineers themselves were responsible for their own accidental death?

    To some extent – yes. No visitor should take undue liberty in an unknown and unfamiliar place without a person belonging to the host organization attending to them. They walked into their own death. Probably, due to lack of familiarity, they could not imagine that the chamber could have been nitrogen fired. By all means, they should have waited for guidance and direction. It appears that they were in a hurry as their visit was at the end of the day.

v. Do you think the families of the visiting engineers would get compensation? From whom?

Yes. The respective families of the visiting engineers who died should get suitable compensation from their own employer organization because they died while discharging their official duties, notwithstanding the fact that they made a few mistakes.

vi. Do you think the employer of the dead engineer will succeed in getting compensation from Murthy's employer?

This is more of a legal than managerial issue. The ultimate outcome will depend more on the dexterity of the respective lawyers engaged by both the parties. Fundamentally, the managerial consideration would be that Murthy's employer did not derive any financial, commercial or economic benefits from the visits of the two engineers in their plant. It was more of a gesture to build up goodwill in the industrial circle, which unfortunately went horribly wrong owing to lapses and mistakes from both the parties involved.

vii. What are the lessons in HRM you draw from this case study?

This case teaches the practitioners and students of HRM quite a few lessons worth learning:

a. The importance of managerial communication: Murthy should have been informed by his own seniors of the visit much in advance. Security's information to Murthy of the visit exactly when it took place gave rise to annoyance and surprise due to lack of any previous information.

b. Time restriction to be imposed on visits by outsiders: The visitors should have been allowed to come in at least two hours before the closure of the shift. Because the time in their hand was short, they made some short cuts and thereby endangering their own lives. They should not have been allowed to visit at the fag end of the day.

c. Security lapses: The security staff should not have allowed the two engineers to come inside the factory without escorts. Had any one of them escorted the visitors straight to Murthy's department, got them introduced to Murthy and then left, this tragedy would not have happened. Murthy was eagerly waiting for them to arrive.

CASE STUDY 3

CORPORATE MARRIAGE BLUES

Sadashiva Shetty, a Chartered Accountant by qualification, is in some way, quite different from his ilk. He had a liking and knack for things technical from his childhood but strangely opted for and studied Commerce from plus two and graduation, capped it up with a CA qualification as if as a finishing touch. He soon had a flourishing practice as financial advisor and external auditor for a number of MSMEs in the industrial estates of his city. One of his clients, a fabrication MSME, a jobbing industry catering to large industries, became sick due to financial constraints. In fact, the industry became sick due the negligence of its two promoters who wished to migrate to the US and was reluctant to infuse more capital the industry needed badly for technology up gradation and capacity expansion.

Shetty grabbed it virtually for a song. He quickly set right the financial issues and put it back on track. He ran it quite well for more than three years but soon after that, his lack of technical expertise came to the fore. After all, the industry was basically technology based. Of course, he hired a few bright technical brains, but everything said and done, these bright boys lacked ownership commitment which was the sine-qua-non of such a technical venture. Finance was the obvious plus point of Shetty's MSME, technology was the only weakness, Shetty's technical knack notwithstanding.

AS if, so to say, at the other end of the spectrum, let us look at Pramod Shanbhog, a bright mechanical engineer form IIT, Madras (today's Chennai) running his own MSME, which has been a brilliant product innovator. Physics and Mathematics had been his pet subjects from the very childhood, no wonder; he took to mechanical engineering like a duck taking to water. Being independent minded, he was, sort of, suffocating in L&T for five years at a junior level. At the threshold of his career advancement to the middle level, he quit and set up his own venture, a MSME in the same industrial estate as Shetty's. Only hitch was that they did not know each other. Of late, Shanbhog had some problems concerning liquidity and cash flow issues and was contemplating to approach a financial advisor.

That hitch was also removed by providence when they bumped into each other in a marriage party in Mangalore, their common native city. Both of them, after a reality check, found light of hope simmering at the end of the proverbial tunnel because their respective weaknesses and strength more or less fully complemented each other or so, they at least, thought. Shetty began camping in Shanbhog's industry for a thorough stock taking of the state of affairs: order book position, stock position, WIP on the line, etc. Balance sheet, as on date, was prepared for both the entities. Shetty's accounting instinct was telling that the EPS of the combined entity would be double of each of them individually, as on date. The combined entity was inaugurated with a great fanfare, but their hopes were short lived.

In fact, when the two hopeful entrepreneurs were chalking out heady days for their combined future, a different story altogether was brewing among the employees of both their enterprises:

- It was rumoured in Shetty's enterprise that Shanbhog's one was starved of cash and was in a dire situation. So, Shetty was rescuing Shanbhog from an impending financial disaster. Hence, they should be treated as underdogs, not equal.
- One of the reasons of Shanbhog,s financial difficulties was his tendency to resort to extensive overtime which Shetty strictly avoids and never allows. Hence, the workers of the erstwhile Shanbhog's factory will earn less.
- Shanbhog's people fondly celebrate their foundation day with fanfare every year. But in Shetty's factory culture, there was no such thing. As Shanbhog's enterprise will no longer exist, the foundation day will also have to be forgotten.

- IT was also rumoured that the technical supervisors of Shanbhog's factory were technically far superior to those of Shetty's, hence in the new entity, they should be the bosses in the supervisory cadre. But, how that can be allowed, just yesterday they were starving.
- Shanbhog was very fond of giving bonus based on wage rates, not linked with profits, Shetty insists on linking bonus with profit strictly. Shanbhog's erstwhile workers are worried, their bonus would vanish.

Because of such wild and widespread rumour mongering, the technical and supervisory personnel of both the merging enterprises started leaving en-masse and the hopeful promoters were looking at a bleak and uncertain future.

Questions:

i. What was the merit of this merger? Was this merger justified?

This merger was justified from the point of view of complementing strengths and weaknesses of both the merging partners. Shetty's enterprise was weak in technical aspects whereas Shanbhog's 'venture apparently lacked in financial prudence. On the surface, this merger made a lot of sense to begin with.

ii. Were the assumptions favouring the idea of merger too simplistic? Were they flawed ab initio? Analyze.

Definitely, as explained in the answer to the previous question, the very idea of merging these two entities made a lot business sense and was not flawed to start with but certain human factors were either not considered as important or were unduly taken for granted.

Financial and technical parameters give the impetus or motivation for mergers, but that is only the so called 'coming together.' Staying together involves matching of value system, culture and attitude of accommodation on the part of both the parties.

iii. What could be the real thorny issues in the background coming onto the way of a smooth merger? Can you identify them?

It is a classic case of human nature prevailing over business sense. Human nature of self-pride, ego, arrogance, false sense of superiority, one up man ship, all these are playing havoc with the success of the joint venture in its implementation. Once there is a marriage between two corporate entities, there will be shaking up in the existing hierarchical structure and new hierarchies emerge with new power equations. Some will lose and some will gain in the bargain, and, of course, the potential losers will oppose the merger tooth and nail.

Also, there is a clash of value system, culture, practices and traditions. This is in addition to the clash of vested interests. Extensive rumour mongering adds fuel to the fire and a sense of uncertainty and insecurity spreads among the employees resulting in their exodus and thereby jeopardizing the very success of the joint venture.

iv. What would be your advice to the two entrepreneurs/promoters to save the industry from any further damage and ensure success of the joint venture?

It appears from the narration of this case that both the entrepreneurs have expertise in their own respective fields but none of them have the holistic perspective of the overall enterprise management incorporating issues pertaining to human resources, human relations and industrial relations. They should immediately hire an external consultant dealing with these areas who should meet all the workers, discuss and enlighten them about the merits of the merger and thereby dispel any doubts, misgivings and speculation about the future.

v. Is this case pertaining to HRM? What lessons in management you derive from this case study?

Marriages are made in heaven but broken across the dining table – so they say. Corporate marriages are made in the board rooms but broken at the grass root levels. This is definitely a case about HRM as the challenge to the management is posed by the employees. It is also an issue involving clash of culture, value system and traditions and thereby introducing elements of OB.

Two business entities may come together to derive positive synergy out of their union in the sense that one entity's weakness is the other entity's strength and vice versa. But people down the line have their own equations, motives, apprehensions and fears. They may lack the spirit of accommodation due to all these. These are the OB challenges in corporate mergers.

To ensure success of the merger, the HR professionals have to take up the challenge of enlightening the people regarding the merit of the merger and how they would be benefited in the long run. They have to be convinced by appropriate communication as to how they will reap the benefits in the future for which some of them may have to put up with temporary inconveniences. So, the success of an otherwise meritorious merger is clinched by the astute HR managers.

CASE STUDY 4

TREASURE AT THE BOTTOM OF THE PYRAMID

Mr. Rajat Malhotra was a typical Delhiite, very much like an American, in some senses. An American in his/her heart of hearts has always a question ringing: what is there in the rest of the world other than the USA? Similarly, a Delhi-walla also often mulls over the question: what is there in the rest of India other than Delhi? This kind of subtle arrogance was the hall mark of Rrajat Malhotra, an alumnus of the prestigious Delhi School of Economics. Personally, for him, of course, such a question was more concerned with his own subject of specialization i.e Economics: "What is there in any subject of study other than Economics, the subject of all subjects?" According to him, the much hallowed management science was nothing but applied Economics with bit of common sense, any other frills touted as management, hardly made any sense to him.

Ironically, he did not land up being an economist, like many of his classmates who joined banks and financial institutions as Economic Advisors. He joined a famous IT firm headquartered in Bangalore as a management trainee, in campus recruitment. He had no regrets, he came up to the middle management cadre very fast, by the fourth year of service, to be precise, by dint of his energy, enthusiasm, smartness, aggressive drive and intelligence. But problems started surfacing soon thereafter. Authorities reposed a lot of faith in him and his style of working. He was made a section head by the time he was barely twenty seven, a sort of record in the whole IT behemoth, even internationally.

Everything was not exactly hunky-dory, however. Dissidence, not in a small scale that too, was growing, mainly because of a few convictions he developed during his service over the years:

* Some will always fall in, some will fall out and some will be indifferent cats on the wall, no matter what you do.

** Trying to satisfy everybody and please everyone is a sure shot recipe for failure.

*** Dissidence is a part of professional life, ignore the ignorant.

These convictions got manifested in whatever he did. He commanded a section of thirteen people and was reporting to the head of the marketing department which had six other sections like his. His section was dedicated to evolve innovative means or even solutions for product promotion. Theirs was a B2B software business and they were facing a few serious challenges posed by the customers.

Addressing one of these thorny issues, he was conducting a meeting with his sub-ordinate officers, of course, as a routine exercise one fine morning:

Rajat "So my friends, that is it. Let us proceed the way I explained and let us hope for the best. Let us sit with the customer's representatives and convince them that we are customizing the products for their sake; in reality, however, the product will be the way we want i.e addressing other customers also, clear?"

Exactly, as per his conviction, he found the audience divided, seven agreed, four did not, another two were just staring at the other two groups and kept mum.

—   "But Sir, I think we should not underestimate our customers, eventually they will see through and we may lose them. Let us have another hard look at the product. We may be able to do justice to what they exactly need." One of the dissidents blurted out and the other three nodded in agreement.

—   Rajat saw red, it was a clear case of insubordination, he thought.

– "Nothing doing my friend, I hope you remember who the boss is." He raised his voice and commanded the other group of seven to call the customer's representative for a meeting the very next day.

The meeting was a disaster, the customer's representatives stuck to their guns. They also threatened; they won't condone any further delay in the delivery. They would sue the supplier for liquidated damages as per the provision of the purchase order. Rajat was crestfallen and decided to take help from his superior i.e the department head, for the first time in his career. He asked for an appointment from his PA.

Within a couple of days, he sat with his senior and explained the situation. The senior gave him a patient hearing as was his wont and asked him not to worry. He called all the subordinates of Rajat in his own chamber and announced a contest. Whoever, an individual or even a group, could find an innovative solution so that the company earns profit, expand its market without antagonizing this particular customer, would be rewarded handsomely i.e. financially and career wise. He gave ten days' time.

Within just seven days, the same dissident group who took a challenge to solve this issue, found out that five of the seven modules of the software this customer ordered for, were identical to an existing product and hence were readily available. Only two modules were required to be custom built within the available time of about three months. The software was delivered within time.

Questions:

i. What was exactly wrong? Was Rajat that bad a manager?

Well, from the narration of the case it appears to be so. Rajat had excellent individual qualities i.e energy, enthusiasm, aggressiveness, capacity for hard work, etc. By virtue of these qualities, he sailed through at a junior position and could impress his seniors. But when he was required to head a team and get things done by others, it was a different ball game. He had to develop interpersonal skills, which he lacked. He should have been a bit more tactful rather than arrogantly throwing his weight around.

ii. Were his convictions out of place? Were they not valid?

His convictions were valid, but not exactly relevant for the interest of the company. He could ignore the ignorant, but how could he, on earth, figure out who was actually ignorant? Just because a few of our colleagues may not agree with us, we can't ignore them. HRM is about maximizing employee engagement. Our approach should be inclusive not exclusive.

iii. Do you think taking recourse to contests, rewards, incentives, etc. are the only viable ways to get things done?

We have learnt from the theories of Douglas McGregor that type X employees are self-motivated and need not be dragged, pressurized or goaded into performing. They perform spontaneously. Type Y employees need these, so it all depends on the types of employees involved. Of course, this type of categorization in most of the organizations is too simplistic. Here, the situation is a bit different, Rajat's dogmatic attitude towards a certain class of subordinates alienated them and their engagement was minimal.

Rajat's senior, by virtue of his experience and maturity, could sense that they were in a crisis situation and he declared incentives to tide over that.

iv. Which other way, you think, such a crisis situation could be avoided?

The company and the team concerned faced a crisis under a boiling situation owing to several managerial lapses. First and foremost, the top management's absolute faith in Rajat's capability was uncalled for. Rajat was given a lot of undue liberty and he used to report to his senior rarely, unless there was a crisis. Secondly, because of the management's over reliance and faith in his capability, Rajat also became overconfident.

Thirdly, Rajat's unforgiving disposition and lack of accommodative attitude towards a section of his sub-ordinates contributed to the crisis.

v. What lesson in OB you derive from this case study?

We can derive several valuable lessons in OB from this case study:

a. Even if an executive is too brilliant, he should not be given out of turn promotion or an undue elevation. Other potent avenues of rewarding should be explored. Giving him power and authority too early should be the last option.

b. Even if an executive gets promoted prematurely because of any managerial indiscretion, there should be strict supervision and vigil over him, immediately after the promotion. The chances of his making mistakes during this period is very high as he takes time to get adjusted to his new role handling higher authority and discharging higher responsibility.

c. There should be more frequent meetings and interactions between the section head and the heads of teams so that any hitch can't develop into a full blown crisis.

d. The section head should have his extended eyes and ears to gather information regarding any misunderstanding, lack of co-operation, ill feeling, bickering among the team members. He can optimally use the channels of informal communication for the same.

e. Rajat should have been sent for a suitable executive development program soon after his elevation and before he takes up higher responsibility.

f. Full employee engagement should always be given top priority. A group of people, however inconvenient, should never be alienated, so that they are not allowed to contribute. They may, as well, handsomely contribute if an appropriate situation is created.

CASE STUDY 5

TRAILING A JUSTIFIABLE DREAM-THAT SUDDENLY APPEARS TOO FAR

Mr. Kanakasekharan was flabbergasted and stupefied by this sudden turn of events, could not quite figure out why it happened only to him. He became an innocent victim of circumstances-so he thought, his conscience was telling him.

He has been a very serious and sincere executive during the last five years in the Germanium department of Semiconductor division of a large electronic industry in Bangalore. Germanium having been outdated, his department was being wound up and all the employees, i.e. workers and executives transferred to Silicon department which was a huge one. As the industry belonged to the Government of India and the employees concerned were permanent, no one was required to lose job due to the obsolescence. But, the exercise, apparently simple, had tremendous HRM implications.

Firstly, all the employees transferred would have to be trained in the new trade. During the training period, their productivity would plummet but their wages and bonus can't; the measure would have serious profitability implication for the division. Secondly, (this is applicable for executives) once an executive is transferred to a new and bigger department, his identity and contribution to the erstwhile smaller department would be obscure and out of reckoning; his promotion prospects and career would be likely to suffer. Kanakasekharan's seniors were well aware of this. As his promotion was due, the seniors decided to complete the promotion formalities before transferring him. The mandatory interview was also over and the order was yet to be released.

On the other hand, in another far away arena, another episode was unfolding in Kanakasekharan's home town in Tamil Nadu. His parents were looking for a suitable match for him. He had advised his parents to look for an educated and working girl that could work and supplement income for the family. Cost of living in Bangalore was significantly higher and one income might not suffice. When his father came to know about his forthcoming promotion, he put off the search for a while, because after the promotion, his son's value in the marriage market would be much higher.

In fine, Kanakasekharan was just in for a double bonanza, but his destiny proved otherwise. Instead of the much awaited promotion with transfer order, what he received was an order of suspension, pending enquiry. A charge of sexual harassment and taking undue advantage of his official position was lodged against him by his colleague, Manjula, a lady supervisor in his team in the former Germanium department. Manjula was a diploma holder in Electronics from a local poly-technique and was about four year's junior to him by age. She put up a written representation to the top management alleging that Kanakasekharan took undue advantage of his seniority and became too intimate to her than what was officially warranted. He had promised to marry her but later ditched her and his parents were looking for a match.

Kanaksekharan was absolutely clear in his conscience. Yes, their intimacy was more than just due, but it was Manjula's own initiative and overture rather than his evil intention that was responsible for that. His modest and conservative upbringing did not permit him to take any undue advantage. He, indeed, was mulling over the idea of marrying Manjula, but when he came to know that Manjula was equally close to a few other male colleagues also in the company, he backed out and Manjula was taking revenge. Now, Kanakasekharan was staring at an uncertain future.

Questions:

    i. Due to technological obsolescence, a particular department/section may have to closed down and the employees rehabilitated if no retrenchment/lay-off is possible in a government industry:

        a. What are the HR challenges involved in the exercise?

The HR challenges are quite daunting. Because nobody can be retrenched or laid off and if they are permanent employee, their seniority has to be maintained intact. If some of the work force are temporary and contractual employees, temporary employees can be terminated and for contractual employees, the contract re-done afresh.

But for permanent employees, due to continuity of service, their seniority has to be maintained, along with seniority, come wage scale, increment and bonus. All these parameters will have to be taken care of as if there has not been any change in their job description and service condition. On the other hand, all the transferred employees will have to be trained extensively in the new trade requiring new skills. The implication is that for quite some time, these transferred employees' contribution and involvement will be far less compared to their wages and bonus. Mitigating these contrasting issues will be quite strenuous for the HR professionals involved.

b. What are the OB challenges involved in this exercise?

The OB challenges are far more formidable. The existing employees and supervisors of silicon department will definitely not welcome the influx of new people who are not expert, not even fully familiar with the technicalities of the departmental work but are bestowed with the same seniority and wages by the management. They will feel that a bunch of inferior people are thrust upon them to accommodate.

So, the co-operation from the people existing in the silicon department will be hard to come by which will, in turn, affect the morale of the workforce coming in. Productivity of both the groups of people will suffer. Ironically, both of them will have grudge against the management. The management will have to sense it and neutralize it with great tact before the discontent does substantial damage to the organization as a whole.

ii. From the limited character sketch of Kanakasekharan, is there any basis to believe that he took undue advantage of his position and let down Manjula?

At the outset, it does not appear to be so i.e Kanakasekharan does not seem to have taken any undue advantage of his official position. When, in an organization young unmarried people are working together, it is but natural that there may be intimacy between any two individuals of the opposite sex by law of nature. There is no evidence to suggest that Kanakasekharan tried to do any undue favour to Manjula, misusing his official position, to acquire intimacy. Both of them being unmarried and in the marriageable age, hunting for life partners, might have found each other compatible and hence the intimacy.

iii. Is there any scope for concluding otherwise? Did Manjula try to take advantage of her official relationship and proximity for her personal life? Such a possibility can't be ruled out. Given to understand that Manjula was close and friendly to a few other male colleagues, probably eligible bachelors, it appears that she was hunting for a suitable life partner within the industry. And that possibility makes quite a bit of sense. She would be familiar with the personal character, qualification, future prospects of her potential groom before tying the knot. That would have been far better than marrying an unknown person which normally happens in an arranged marriage. But, trying to tarnish, malign and jeopardize the career of an old flame would be a serious issue.

iv. Can this case come under the purview of sexual harassment?

Yes, it can as well come. The authorities in charge of adjudicating over this issue should be mature, understanding human nature, compassionate, empathetic, sensitive and discrete to settle the issue impartially. On one hand, the career prospects of an innocent executive (as has been made out in this case) is at stake, if he is really without blemish. On the other hand, the sensibilities, dignity and personal integrity of a young woman are also under scanner. So, the authorities have to tread very carefully. It is really a formidable challenge for them.

v. What are the lessons you derive from this case study as far as a) HR is concerned b) OB is concerned?

a. For HR, the entire case poses a huge challenge. It touches upon almost the entire gamut of HR functions like transfer, promotion, training and development, fixing compensation, performance bonus, employee engagement, keeping employee morale high and unperturbed, receiving complaints, constituting board of enquiry and adjudication. Justice has to be done to both Kanakasekharan and Manjula and their personal reputation protected.

b. As far as OB is concerned, when the employees of both the sexes are working together, such issues may crop up and there should be proper and prior arrangement in place to deal with them as per the provisions of the 'sexual harassment at work place' act. For the employees who are transferred to a new division, behavioral issues would crop up regarding seniority, competence and compensation disparity and they have to be handled deftly.

CASE STUDY 6

A TRIAL AT THE WUTHERING HEIGHTS AND THE SUBSEQUENT CAREER PLUNGE INTO THE ABYSS

Ravi Nayak was in the seventh heaven before literally going up the hills. Today, his past three years of dedicated labour will be tested by the touch stone of field trials involving the customers i.e. the Indian Army. Ravi Nayak, all of twenty nine years, an alumnus of NIT, Surathkal and hailing from Mangalore in Karnataka, joined Asian Electronics at the tender age of twenty three years just after completing his graduation in Electronics and Communication Engineering. After the mandatory one year training as probationer, he got posted in a team of six engineers developing a multi-channel communication equipment for the Indian Army. One specific qualitative requirement of the equipment was that it had to be a rugged all weather equipment meant for rough and uneven terrain conditions prevailing particularly in the border state of Jammu and Kashmir.

A big contingent of Army jawans, headed by a few JCOs i.e. the actual users in the Signals regiment posted at the borders has congregated at Bangalore, the manufacturing company's headquarter, to have a firsthand exposure and familiarity with the equipment they are going to use henceforth in their border postings. Ministry of Defense needed the feedback from the actual users before giving the green signal to go ahead with the manufacture in a mass scale. The resultant potential order expected would run into several hundred crores for several years to come which would provide the bread and butter for the equipment division of Asian Electronics for quite some time to come. Career growth prospect for the entire team of engineers working for the project also depended on it s success and the whole team including Ravi was well aware of this.

Ravi was instructed by his boss, the departmental head, to book a factory bus, load the entire contingent of jawans and JCOs, the equipment and the supporting hardware with erection accessories and travel to Nandi Hills, a popular tourist spot of hilly terrain about sixty kilometers away from Bangalore. The Department of Telecommunication (DoT) has been maintaining a microwave relay station on the top of Nandi Hills, permission had been obtained to install the trial station in their premises just for a day. The other station would be located on the roof top of the R & D building of Asian Electronics campus. Everything seemed well planned. Immediately after breakfast, the flock started the journey from the factory. Almost at the peak of the hill, near the DoT establishment, there is a Shiva temple. Ravi thought it appropriate to offer puja before commencing the trial, requesting divine intervention for the success of the trial.

And, their prayer was granted, the trial went off very smoothly and successfully. Capability and credibility of Ravi, his group of engineers and the equipment became ingrained as the user group was happy with the communication set up between the two stations. They managed to believe that such equipments would be useful at the border areas. But there was something more sinister to follow. When they were about to wind up after the evening coffee, suddenly, the sky got overcast with thick clouds and before they could realize anything, it started pouring heavily. The whole hill top was engulfed in gusty winds and it became intensely cold; everybody started shivering. Ravi waited patiently for the rain to stop but for over a couple of hours or so, there was no sign of it.

The bus driver got impatient and warned Ravi that once it became dark, it would be difficult to drive as there might be minor landslides here and there. As there was no time to pack up the elaborate hardware and load on the bus, leaving the entire installation overnight at the custody of the DoT staff was imminent. But, neither Ravi nor the DoT staff had permission for the same. Ravi, in a terrible dilemma, had to contact his boss for the second time. During the first call of the day, he was congratulated, this time he was told sternly that even the boss did not have the authority to permit costly defense materials to be left overnight at the custody of unauthorized persons. The DoT staff present at the spot understood Ravi's predicament, but echoed the same helplessness i.e the lack of authority.

Desperate and driven to the wall by the turn of events, Ravi decided to take his own risk to leave the station hardware at the DoT shelter for the night and came back empty handed. He had to make several subsequent visits to Nandi hills to recover back all the materials; nothing was lost except, of course, his own career. He was charge sheeted and suspended for alleged dereliction of duty, overstepping his authority etc. That became an indelible black mark in his career. Once an executive gets suspended, he can't be considered for promotion when due, unless six months have elapsed since the suspension gets revoked. He started looking for an alternative employment.

Questions:

1. Was the management justified in suspending Ravi?

   Well, it appears that there was no other alternative at management's disposal under the circumstances. The rules and regulations prevailing at the time were simply not comprehensive enough to consider and take adequate care of all the eventualities that could arise when costly equipments are taken outside the factory for customer trials. Management went strictly by the rule book, instead, they could have used their discretion.

2. Was Ravi's action justified under the circumstances?

   It is really difficult to find fault with what Ravi did. The situation was very desperate and he had no other alternative. He did his best possible and sensible under those adverse circumstances. He displayed remarkable presence of mind but, unfortunately, there was no provision for his actions under the rules and hence he had to be punished.

3. Had you been in the position of Ravi, what else you would have done?

   At the first place, before going on trials by taking the costly factory properties with me, I would have gone through the relevant rules and regulations thoroughly. Moreover, after the heavy thunder shower, when there was no way of carrying the equipments back to factory, I could have sent back my colleagues to the factory by the bus and I myself stayed back in the DOT establishment with its own security staff for the night, guarding the movable properties. The very next morning, I could have gone back to the factory carrying all the items. After cross checking with our own security that all the items had come back, I could have sent a detailed report detailing what had happened and justifying my action, of course, endorsed and forwarded by my immediate superior and the Head of the Department, to the top management and thereby facilitating their use of discretion.

4. Is it a matter pertaining to HRM or OB? What lessons you can learn from this case study?

Though, at the very outset, it appears to be a case in the area of operations management, it has got tremendous HR implications. An intelligent, sincere and by all means competent engineer who successfully clinched order for the company and is an asset to the company is getting suspended, pending enquiry, instead of getting rewarded and now contemplating leaving the company. It is a tragedy of its own kind.

All these are because of inadequacy in the scope, coverage and provisions in the relevant rules and regulations regarding field trials of equipments for the customer/s. If the equipments are carried outstation for trials, they need not be brought back on the same day and their safety will be the responsibility of the engineer in charge of trials. Such trials may continue for even several months. When the items are taken out of the factory but not out of station, they have to be brought back by the same night. There was no provision in the rules covering the exigencies of circumstances under which the items could not be brought back despite due diligence on the part of the participants.

This shortcoming in provisioning is mainly due to lack of coordination and communication between the operation and HR personnel. The exigencies may arise in the areas of operations about which the HR people who framed the rules have no clear idea. Cross functional communication is a must while framing the rules for adequate provisioning and coverage before fixing penalty for any violations.

DISCIPLINE VERSUS CREATIVITY, DILIGENCE VERSUS BRILLIANCE-WHICH WAY TO GO?

There was celebration in the air and quite rightly so. The engineers in the department of R & D VII, in the Development and Engineering division of M/s Asian Electronics Ltd., Bangalore were in cloud nine and they deserved it. The Indian Air Force (IAF) has placed an order for a pilot batch of 500 sets of Ground to Air, UHF, Synthesiser Controlled, and Multichannel communication equipment that the department had recently developed. The IAF, for once, has not been a customer easy to impress and convince. They had conducted extensive field trials in all sorts of adverse climatic conditions in Shillong, Jamnagar, Jaishalmer, Chandigarh and even Ladhakh. The equipment did not let the designers down. It never failed.

The feat was definitely a feather in the cap of R & D VII and more so for its HoD, Mr. Chandak, an Electronics graduate from the College of Engineering, Pune. He was one of the youngest DGM the organization had and was going to be its youngest and brightest AGM also. With a bit of luck, he would also make it to the Director, R & D, or so, everybody thought. There was, however, another unprecedented challenge lurking just ahead, he realized a little later.

Recognition from the management soon followed thereafter. Mr. Chandak felt that the management was being a bit more than just generous. As the first step, management gifted, all and sundry, without discrimination, Titan wrist watches, worth about Rs. 5000/, each with the company's loge imprinted on the dial. Everybody put on broad smiles, except, of course, the core team members who developed the equipment. Mr. Chandak felt the heat, six members put on long faces, "Reward to everybody is recognition to nobody" – an engineer was grumbling to another, Mr. Chandak overheard. But, he had more problems in the pipeline, the second instalment of the reward and recognition was even more devastating.

This time, Mr. Chandak took the initiative and met the Executive Director and explained the problem. ED assured him the management was happy not only with the core team but with the whole department for the overall climate conducive to creativity and discipline that Mr. Chandak had developed and maintained in the department. The second instalment of the reward would be meant for the team proper. It was, he said, Mr. Chandak's prerogative to identify engineers who were to be rewarded, and recommend, without his recommendation, no reward would be given. Mr. Chandak was required to identify the engineers whose promotion was due and they would be promoted immediately. And those for whom the next promotion, as per the company's rules and practices, was not due and far off, would be given two advanced increment with two years' seniority.

Now, Mr. Chandak was in a real dilemma. He was a strict disciplinarian and was inclined to believe that sense and observance of discipline was the most important and desirable quality among engineers and no amount of knowledge and competence in the subject, however up to date and creative, will suffice if discipline was not there. Out of the six engineers in the team, the most brilliant was a mechanical engineer who designed the front panel and the housing cabinet of sturdy aluminium mould which provide, apart from the required mechanical strength against vibration, high visibility, accessibility and hence serviceability. IAF was impressed by its sturdy look.

But, Francis George, the mechanical engineer we are talking about, would appear for duty every Monday morning smelling alcohol and burnt tobacco, indicating that he had a jolly good time in the previous Sunday evening. Another prodigious electronics man was Abid Hussain whose flawless design of the heart of the electronic system i.e the digital synthesiser took away everybody's breathe. Yet, according to the HoD Chandak, he had a serious problem. Every Friday afternoon he won't be available in the department for religious reasons which the HoD is not exactly happy about. Yet another electronic whiz kid was Dhanasekharan from Madurai. His contribution, the transmission system was so superb that even in the rugged terrains of Ladhakh, the synchronous system maintained the link intact, no ordinary feat. Once again, the IAF was impressed. But, his problem was, he hopped to Madurai every now and then to conduct the annual ceremonies of his numerous ancestors throughout the year.

All these symptoms were due to serious lack of professionalism, so Chadak thought and did not recommend their promotions which fell due. When the other three mediocre, but the so called disciplined sentinels received their advance increments, those three creative geniuses put in their papers. R & D VII had to be dismantled, the remaining three engineers distributed to other departments and Chandak was transferred to one of the production divisions of the company where he was feeling like a fish out of water.

Questions:

    i.   How do you justify the success of the equipment designed in R & D VII?

        Notwithstanding the elements of indiscipline and lack of dedication, the engineers in the design team were talented and it speaks volume of the capacity and competence of the HoD Mr. Chandak who could motivate them and extract a brilliant piece of work from them. It only goes to strengthen the management concept that with the right kind of motivation, talented people can bring their talents together and produce miraculous results. The motivation here, of course, was career advancement and monetary incentives which the management granted as a policy.

    ii.   Do you support the HoD's view about discipline and creativity?

        It goes without saying that a sense of discipline, if used with discretion, can facilitate a creative contribution but discipline for the sake of it, cannot foster, create, promote creativity by itself. If there is creative talent already inherent in someone, discipline can contribute to conversion of that creative talent into tangible results for everyone to see. If an individual lacks in creative talents, by virtue of being disciplined, can't acquire that quality. Creative talents in individuals should be identified, nurtured, encouraged and suitably rewarded and any accompanying traits of indiscipline should be ironed out by extensive counselling, not punishment.

iii. Do you think creative people are inherently undisciplined and vice versa? By and large, it has been observed to be so. Creative people, in general, are disorderly and lack discipline, because orderliness and regulation restrict their creative spirit from flourishing. Highly creative people are governed by a different value system. They always question the status quo; they get restless and impatient with what exists and taken for granted, think out of the box for doing things newly and differently. In the bargain, they may have to sacrifice neatness, appearance, orderliness and discipline which they don't mind. But, the reverse is not true, i.e. all people who are disorderly and undisciplined, need not be creative.

Moreover, creative people are inherently undisciplined not by design, but by default. They can't manage creativity and discipline together. Sometimes, they are not even aware that they lack discipline but when pointed out, they prefer creativity to discipline.

iv. Had you been the HoD, how you would have managed the situation? If I were the HoD, at first, I would have identified the creative individuals under my control and supervision and observe them. If any one of them is found to be lacking in discipline, orderliness, dedication and commitment, I would have taken recourse to extensive counselling by professional industrial counsellors hired for the purpose. Sometimes, a creative individual becomes undisciplined and disengaged inadvertently when the working atmosphere and climate are not conducive to creativity. He becomes bored and tired with the working conditions and co-workers' negative attitude to creativity and loses interest in work which manifests itself into lack of commitment. As a senior, I would have ensured that an atmosphere and climate conducive to and encouraging creativity are maintained in the department.

v. What lessons in management you derive from this case study?

The management lessons that this case teaches us, can be summarised as follows:

a. In society as well as in workplace, people are made of strengths and weaknesses and hardly anybody is an exception to that.

b. Both these strengths and weaknesses are to be identified and treated/handled separately by separate means. These two means should never be mixed up and confused with each other.

c. After birth and throughout their upbringing, people develop different value systems depending upon their parental background, religion, culture, society etc. They come from diverse places and communities to work to earn their livelihood. Once in an organization, organizational value system will be imposed on them and they have to make room for and get adjusted to that as early as possible for their own benefit and growth. Nevertheless, an individual may not be able to sacrifice his entire individual value system to the altar of the organization if the climate and culture demand that and different people will get adjusted to this value adjustments differently. Every organization and its management should respect this uniqueness of individuals and make allowance for that.

d. It is incumbent upon every manager to identify strengths and weaknesses of people who are with him and to figure out how they can be adjusted to the benefits of both the organization and the individual. Every strength should be strengthened further and weaknesses overcome as far as possible. But, strengths are more important than weaknesses.

e. Every individual and collective contribution to the mission of the organization, however small, should be recognized and rewarded. Nobody's contribution should be ignored and overlooked under the pressure of his weakness however overwhelming and strong.

CASE STUDY 8

COMPASSION UNLIMITED

Mr. Rajan is a highly dedicated professional and a strict disciplinarian. He is the HR manager of Matrix Pvt. Ltd, a SSI registered under the MSME Act 2006. Matrix, a five year old company, has been promoted by five young technocrat entrepreneurs who are all graduate mechanical engineers with about a decade of industrial experience in fabrication. Matrix has been a vendor to several large scale manufacturing industries around Chennai city.

Mr. Rajan is the head of HR functions in Matrix and has a problem in hand. Mr. Jacob Pandian, the most experienced and skilled machinist that Matrix has, has not been reporting for duty for the last more than three months without leave or notice. Jacob is the fittest case for termination. Several show – cause notices sent by registered post have come back undelivered with the message 'door locked.' Jacob's residence, as per the records of the company, is located in a lower middle class suburb of Chennai.

Out of the workforce of seventy nine workers that Matrix has, only nine are super machinist and Jacob is the best of them. He does not have a formal technical degree or diploma; neither has he cared to know much about the rules and regulations of service. But when an intricate machining job is ordered, his name comes first in reckoning. Mr. Rajan, though not a technical person himself, quite well understands the implication of Jacob's departure but can't help it. He identified a few workers residing nearby Jacob's residence in the city and sent them for enquiry, but to no avail. The door is locked and the neighbours are not aware where Jacob and his wife could be. As per the records of the company, Jacob was childless.

As meticulous as he could be, Mr. Rajan consulted a lobour lawyer, discussed the issue and got a masterpiece of a termination letter drafted, keeping all the legal safeguards for the company. He did not have the authority to sign; only the CMD Mr. Akash Gupta has. So, with Jacob's personal records' file in hand, he walks in to Mr. Gupta's chamber.

- Good morning Rajan Saab. What brings you to me in the early morning?
- Very good morning, Sir. Please sign Pandian's termination letter.
- Termination? Why? Are we here to terminate livelihood of people, that too, of a brilliant worker like Jacob Mr. Rajan?
- We can't help it, Sir. He has been absconding for the last more than three months and as per our company's rules –
- Yes, I am very much aware of both his unauthorized absence and the rules, but I remember to have told you to find out the reasons last time when we met and discussed the issue. Have you-
- I sent half a dozen people to his residence; neither he nor any information is available.
- Did you ever venture personally? (Rajan was fuming inside, which HR rule says that a HR manager has to go to a delinquent worker's home personally?). OK; I have understood, I myself will go, give me his address.

The very next day, Gupta was at Jacob's's door and on finding it locked, visits the local municipal office to locate the house owner. The next hour, he was with the owner. He discovers that Jacob's wife had been admitted to the CMC hospital, Vellore and needs an emergency surgery. Jacob has not paid the house rent for the last three months and has been camping by his wife's bed side in the CMC. Gupta collected the ward and bed number details of Jacob's wife and left for Vellore; within a few hours, he was with Jacob at his wife's bed side.

Jacob was overwhelmed seeing the top boss at the hospital and was in tears. He told Gupta that his wife needed immediately a surgery and he was struggling to get the funds needed. Gupta's next job was cut out. He gets back to Matrix, meets and sits with the Finance Director, gets the funds released, to be ratified by the BoD subsequently, hands over the money to Jacob at Vellore. He did not forget to take Rajan with him while handing over the money.

By the next month, Jacob is back to work and his wife to home. Jacob's dedication to Matrix has multiplied since then. Nevertheless, the BoD advised Rajan to get a loan document signed by Jacob, the amount was given interest free to be adjusted from salary during the coming three years. The loan was shown documented/recorded as a loan on compassionate/medical ground, as an 'one-off case 'without involving policy issues of the company.

Questions:

i. Was Mr. Rajan, the HR Manager, right in his approach from the points of view of norms, rules, regulations governing HR practices?

No. Mr. Rajan could not be faulted, at least, on this count. For a SSI like Matrix, which is not a government industry, if any worker absents himself without leave, notice or intimation for as long as three months continuously, he deserves a show cause notice. If the reply to the notice is improper/unacceptable to the management or is not forthcoming at all within fifteen days, he deserves to be terminated. In this case, Jacob could not be served the notice as he was not traceable. So, on the face of it, the stern measure about to be taken by Rajan, though harsh, was justified.

ii. Was there any professional negligence on the part of Mr. Rajan?

As per the rule book, no but if seen from the humanitarian and compassionate ground, yes. And from humanitarian angle, a HR manager should go beyond his rule book, at times, to retain and preserve talents within the organization as and when the situation demands it. He should walk that extra mile to make a difference as this classic case study demonstrates. This home truth was understood by the CEO Mr. Gupta but not by Rajan, quite possibly because of lack of commitment. This case study clearly shows that as a CEO, and also one of the founders, Mr. Gupta was more committed to the welfare of his company and the workers than Rajan who was a hired professional.

iii. Was Mr. Gupta's overtures justified? What can be the implication of his action as far as Matrix is concerned? Consider from all possible angles.

Considering from Mr. Gupta's personal angle, his kind, proactive and compassionate behavior might bring a good lot of personal satisfaction, but considering all the possible implications, his overture can prove both beneficial and harmful for the company in short and long run. In the short run, it will create a lot of goodwill among the work force that they would not be left high and dry in the hours of dire need and their employer would be there to take adequate care for them, sometime out of the way. It would give them a tremendous moral boost.

On the other hand, there is possibility of a morale hazard for the company in the sense that a few unscrupulous workers can take undue advantage of the company's kindness and create a desperate situation for themselves either deliberately or carelessly with the faith that, after all, the employer is always there to bail them out. To safeguard the company's interest in such a situation in future, the company recorded the episode as an 'one-off' so as not to create a precedent and a tradition.

iv. What happens if the BoD of Matrix does not ratify the CEO Mr. Gupta's decision and action?

It is, of course, by all means, the board's prerogative to ratify the CEO's such a situational overture or not. If it is ratified, the arrangement will be as described i.e considering the expenditure as an interest free loan as a welfare measure to be recovered in installments from the salary payable in future. If it is not ratified, the amount will be treated as a personal donation by the CEO without binding the company any way and the amount to be recovered from the CEO's salary.

v. What lessons you derive from this case study as a student of management? The management lessons this case teaches us can be summarized as:

a. The extent to which a professional can stretch himself depends on the direness/exigencies of the situation and his commitment to the organization more than his commitment to the profession.

b. When a professional extends his actions in a dire situation more than what is exactly called for by his professional code of conduct or ethics in the interest of the organization, he may create both opportunities and challenges for the organization concerned. The company, in turn, has to take advantage from the opportunities and to generate sufficient safeguard from the challenges.

c. A hired professional is more committed to his profession rather than any specific organization whereas a promoter will be committed more to the organization he promotes rather than any specific area of profession.

CASE STUDY 9

THE HEART BREAK MESS

Mr. Shambashiva Murthy was residing with his parents in Adyar in today's Chennai before he got a job in Bangalore. Murthy's Telugu speaking forefathers settled in the city of erstwhile Madras in the integrated Madras province during British rule. By virtue of his ancestry, he is fluent in both Tamil and Telugu, south India's two most important languages. After migrating to Bangalore, he has been a bit uncomfortable as he feels he should have at least a moderate command in another south Indian language i.e. Kannada. But, it was taking time for him.

Murthy has been a hardworking and intelligent boy and got a merit seat in government engineering college, at Guindy. He graduated with distinction in Electronics and Communication Engg, and immediately got a job in Asian Electronics Ltd, Bangalore, the biggest electronic equipment maker and supplier to the Indian armed forces. By dint of his diligence and devotion to work, he soon became a favorite of his higher ups. He was included in the elite team of engineers designing and developing an UHF Multichannel Communication equipment for the Indian army to be used in the border. In the meanwhile, Asian Electronics has handsomely rewarded him by deputing him to IIT, kharagpur for postgraduate study in Radar and Communication. Murthy's problems started soon thereafter as he came back from higher studies.

The first prototype of the equipment was developed and Murthy was entrusted with the field trial to be conducted at the special signal regiment, Dhaula Kuan, at the outskirts of New Delhi, NCR. With great enthusiasm and pride as a designer, Murthy flew with the prototype to Delhi and reported to Major Gaurav kapoor, in charge of field trials at the regiment. But, within a few days after the commencement of the trial, Murthy started feeling extremely uncomfortable. His discomfiture and predicament were mounting on several counts.

Firstly, there were issues of food habit and language. Murthy felt that the regiment was situated in a god forsaken and deserted place with no proper food i.e. suitable for his test, available nearby. Even enquiring about the existence of a food stall within the walk able distance was extremely difficult owing to the language barrier as most of the people outside and around the regiment was barely literate. Secondly, Murthy was lodged in the YMCA youth hostel near Parliament Street at the heart of the city; the regiment was located more than twenty kilometers away. As Murthy was new to the city, he was not aware of the public transport facility available and had to depend upon auto rickshaws. Autos were charging exorbitantly including return fares which was a severe strain on Murthy's daily allowances. He could not even argue or negotiate with them because of the language barrier. In order to avoid getting late, Murthy had to skip shaving early in the morning but Major Kapoor did not take this omission very kindly. He politely but firmly told Murthy that nobody should report unshaven to the army establishment as it was against army rules.

- But, Sir, I am a civilian, why should I be governed by army rules? Asked Murthy.
- Any civilian who has been deputed to the army establishment for official duty should follow army rules.-Countered Major Kapoor.
  Murthy felt insulted and took it as a severe infringement on his personal liberty. But, that was just the beginning. To overcome the food problem, Murthy requested Major Kapoor to allow him to take lunch at the army officers' mess located inside the regiment and the Major reluctantly agreed. But, he could use the facility only once. On the second day, he was not allowed to enter the mess and was informed that his pay and perks from Asian Electronics were lower than the junior most army officers' salary and he was not considered equivalent to an officer hence was not eligible to enter officers' mess. However, the army was kind enough to arrange for his lunch at the JCOs' mess. Murthy took this episode as a deadly blow to his self-respect.

There was a silver lining, nevertheless, as the sub-unit designed by Murthy was working magnificently and Asian Electronics was confident of bagging the commercial order after, of course, the equipment proved its worth in the actual field trials at the border areas.

One fine morning in the regimental barrack, Lt. Colonel Rohit Saxena, the commanding officer of the regiment, walked in the trial and evaluation area to have a firsthand glimpse of the equipment functioning. It was a surprise visit and all the officers present in the arena stood up and saluted, except, of course, Murthy. "If the army does not know how to respect me, why should I respect them?" – he thought within himself. But, the army did not take it very kindly. Murthy's misdemeanor and breach of protocol was reported to his higher ups in Asian Electronics. Murthy was called back to Bangalore, suspending the trials.

Murthy took the early morning flight at 6:30 AM and by the lunch time, he was at the Asian Electronics' officers' canteen to take lunch. He found to his shocking surprise, a slew of army jawans in uniforms sitting comfortably and eating their lunch. That was the last straw that broke the camel's back.

The next morning, Shri Chandrasekharan, GM, R & D summoned Murthy in his office and was getting ready to pounce on him. Murthy did not give him that opportunity. He took out a piece of paper from his folder he was carrying and handed over to the boss.

– Here is my resignation, Sir. Please release me at the earliest.

The GM, without losing his composure, lifted the phone and called the concerned HR Manager and asked him to come immediately to his office carrying Murthy's personal file.

– We can't release him, Sir. He is under service bond, we sponsored his higher studies at IIT, he has to pay compensation. –told the HR manager.

Murthy took a bus to Chennai in the same night to visit his father at Adyar. He prevailed upon his aged father, a retired person surviving on his life savings, to help him with the money and the father agreed. Murthy came back to his parents, bag and baggage, and joined an engineering college as an Assistant Professor with almost the same salary within walking distance from his home. He could pay back his dues to his father within a few years.

But for Asian Electronics, the matter turned from bad to worse. The suspended trial could not be resumed as Asian Electronics could not find a suitable replacement within a reasonable time. Ministry of Defense asked the company to transfer the design on 'as is where is' basis to HAL, Hyderabad. It was learnt that HAL, Hyderabad got the commercial order worth several hundred crores ultimately.

Questions:

i. Who can be held responsible for the misadventure, Murthy, Asian Electronics or the Army? Can any one entity, out of these three, be singled out?

Well, it is not that easy to point out who was exactly on the wrong side as far as this case is concerned. All these three entities were right within their respective restricted domains. But nothing went right when they interacted, for a productive purpose, among one another. Let us look at the three entities individually.

Murthy, being out and out a southerner, by birth and upbringing, was not at all familiar with the language and food habit of the northern people and being from a civilian family, not accustomed to army norms and practices. The Indian army, being a military combatant force, has their own rigid rules and regulations befitting their requirements which they don't relax for the sake of anybody for that matter. Only Asian Electronics, the intermediary between these two entities at its two ends and also assumed to have been familiar with both the cultures and practices i.e. civilian and military, should have taken up the cudgels and resolved the conflict which it apparently did not do to its own peril.

ii. What are the respective roles of these three entities that resulted in this mishap?

On the part of Murthy, his ignorance and lack of familiarity with other language, cultures and practices, his intolerance and to some extent immaturity went against him in spite of his tremendous technical competence and success. Tolerance and patience are great virtues even for a genius.

For the army, its rigidity while enforcing its rules and regulations for the sake of discipline and extending those norms to and enforcing on the civilians interacting with them but not trained and familiar with the norms to abide by. Allowances should be there to accommodate minor and inadvertent violations by civilians who the army has to interact with in their own interest.

For Asian Electronics who lost the order despite its technical success and initiative, was apparently indifferent to the issue which called for proactive measures to resolve.

iii. Who is really at the losing end out of these three entities?

Obviously, it was Asian Electronics and quite rightly so. Army got its equipment from another supplier from its own ministry; Murthy got back his earnings albeit from a different discipline in his native city, only Asian Electronics lost the huge order due to its own HR blunder.

iv. Do you think Asian Electronics should/could have acted more pro-actively to prevent this damage to their commercial interest?

Yes, definitely. The company should have been more alert and vigilant regarding the wellbeing, both mental and physical, of one of their engineers whom they had sent out to far off and unfamiliar place for equipment trials. There should have been regular interaction over phone between Murthy and his immediate boss regarding day to day progress and any other issues pertinent to the success of the trial. Murthy could, thus, have got opportunities to explain his predicament before the issue could snowball into a point of no return. No such thing was done.

v. Is it a HR case at all? What is the role of HR in this entire episode?

Yes, indeed, it is one hundred percent a case in HR. Murthy should have been briefed, counseled and trained thoroughly before being sent for the trial. HR functionaries in the company should have advised Murthy's boss regarding the same. Then the company would not have lost him.

SPIRITUAL ENLIGHTENMENT IN ORGANIZATIONAL FRAMEWORK AND ITS REWARDS

Shri Velayudhan Nair was becoming more and more incorrigible; at least, that was what Mr. V.G. patil, Nair's senior officer was thinking. Shri Nair, hailing from Trichur in central Kerala, was a graduate electrical engineer and joined the design department about two decades back. He was in his mid-forties and holding the senior most rank in the middle management level, due for promotion to the higher management cadre. Mr. Patil should be instrumental in getting that promotion to Nair as his immediate senior but it was appearing increasingly impossible. Patil really regretted it. He felt helpless and not without valid reasons.

Shri Nair had been a brilliant design engineer to start his career and simultaneously was deeply religious. He was a great devotee of Lord Guruvayurappan and insisted on visiting the famous temple of the Lord near Trichur, at least once in a quarter, come what may. "Nothing wrong in being religious" – Patil thought, nevertheless, for everything there is a limit even for religiousness. Nair was becoming more and more detached from the material world; was getting entrenched into spirituality. The proverbial icing on the cake was his recent visit to Haridwar and Hrishikesh. Firstly, it was his first visit to the northern part of the country, that too, to the citadel of Hinduism. Secondly, he was, kind of, mesmerized and transformed after listening to some religious discourses by a few revered Gurujis in those holy places.

After coming back from the pilgrimage, he was a completely transformed person, could not concentrate on his project and its progress. In the 'project progress review' meetings, instead of asking the young engineers in his group about the achievements of project targets, he was asking about their spiritual progress and the project was suffering. Mr. Patil, as the head of the department, was observing all these and was cursing Nair as well as his own fate. How could he recommend such a delinquent candidate for a berth in the higher management cadre? And the matter would not end there-Patil thought. If Nair did not get promotion, it would be anything but a feather in Patil's cap and his own promotion to the rank of GM and the divisional head would be jeopardized.

As he was at his wit's end, he met his divisional head and discussed the issue. The divisional head was about to retire, he took the issue philosophically. He advised Patil not to bother much about strays who could not be promoted. He also assured Patil that even through Nair could not be promoted owing to his own limitation, he, as a divisional head, would definitely recommend Patil's promotion to the 'Board of Directors.' Patil was anything but happy and felt that he, as a senior, should not leave Nair to his own fate. He also had a conviction that it was a managerial challenge and he must and should find a befitting solution. He raised the level of his approach, of course, with the divisional head's permission as per protocol and met the Executive Director (ED), in charge of the whole factory.

The ED was on his mettle and advised Patil not to get worked up with Nair's promotion. Just before Nair's first chance of promotion became due as per seniority, he was transferred to the 'Centre for Training and Development' (CTD), the centralized training division for the whole factory. The ED personally found time to sit with Nair, asked him not to worry but design and deliver preliminary to advanced courses on spirituality to the various ranks in the executive cadre. Thenceforth, spirituality and self-actualization became recognized items of training for the development of middle and higher cadre executives as a company policy. Even the company went to the extent of inviting spiritual leaders from the famed ISKCON to deliver series of lectures for the executives.

Nair rose to the occasion, proved his caliber and today he heads the CTD.

Questions:

i. Do you really believe Nair's straying into spirituality was a shortcoming? Can spirituality be termed as delinquency?

Of course not; spirituality, by itself, can' be termed as shortcoming or delinquency or even weakness. Spirituality, by all means, is a quality. But everything said and done, in a corporate setup, everyone has to contribute materially to the survival and growth of the entity in which they are employed. Spirituality definitely elevates the soul individually. But collectively, if it distracts attention from the organization's objectives, it may be viewed as delinquency by the powers that be.

ii. Do you believe, like Mr. Patil that spirituality among executives is a distraction?

Spirituality, by itself, can't be a distraction. But, coming under its spell, if an executive starts contributing less to the organization's objectives to which he is committed, spirituality can be considered a distraction. On the other hand, spirituality can be given a divine dimension even in the organizational framework. The organization should make pursuing superordinate goals one of its objectives and then spirituality can contribute to that goal handsomely. It is up to the powers that be that are in charge of framing objectives, both short and long terms.

iii. Why Mr. Patil was not satisfied with the solution suggested by the divisional head even when his own promotion was assured?

Mr. patil was quite right in remaining dissatisfied even when his own promotion was assured. A superior executive, true to his salt, will aim at not only his own but also his own sub-ordinate/junior executive's career growth as equally important. Mr. Patil felt, and quite rightly so, he would fail in discharging his responsibility as a senior when his own junior officer is denied promotion. It only goes to show that Mr. Patil was a conscientious man and not greedy for his own promotion only. Such executive are, indeed, assets to an organization, as this case study also shows.

iv. What lessons in organizational behavior you derive from this case study? This case study can be taken and viewed as an example of the well-known Maslow's hierarchy of needs pertaining to motivation. Mr. Nayar, without his own knowledge and awareness, got elevated, albeit internally, to the highest level of needs i.e. self-actualization quite unlike his other colleagues who were still dabbling in the fourth stage i.e esteem needs. This phenomenon is nothing uncommon in organizational set up where senior executives often get caught up in the fourth stage and never make it to the fifth during their whole career. Well-crafted training for their development and spiritual progress may help.

A SMALL CHARITY AT A PUBLIC PLACE AND ITS UNWANTED AFTERMATH

Nivedita Garg was a young and intelligent woman at her early twenties, twenty three, to be precise. She was born and brought up in Meerut city, the largest urban agglomeration in western Uttar Pradesh bordering Uttarakhand. Both her parents were in teaching profession, father a college professor and mother a school teacher. Her only elder sibling, her brother was an alumnus of NDA and an army Major now. Hers was a very cultured family of higher values. Her mother was offering free tuition to slum children in her spare times. Her father also identified brilliant but poor students in Meerut, offered them free tuition and guidance. Nivedita also imbibed a good lot of such values from her parents.

Nivedita completed her graduation in Commerce and then MBA in marketing from a renowned management institute in Meerut. She was campus selected by a reputed marketing company headquartered in Chandigarh. She cleared the preliminary screening and was required to appear at the final selection interview in that city. While planning for her journey, out of about half a dozen feasible routes, she decided to catch a bus from Meerut to New Delhi and then catch a train from New Delhi to Chandigarh. She targeted Shatabdi Express starting at 8 AM and reaching Chandigarh by a bit after 11 AM. She could appear at the interview immediately after lunch on the same day.

On that day, she reached New Delhi railway station well within time, rushed to the ticket counter and stood in the queue. When she got the ticket, it was already nick of time. While rushing to the platform, she saw a gentleman, presumably in his late forties or early fifties, in suit, boot and tie, very distinguished looking, walking ahead of her. A lean, hungry and emaciated man, also in his fifties, was following him asking for alms. The beggar also had two children with him, equally lean and hungry, seemed to have not eaten for days. The man was crying and begging for money to feed his children. Nothing new, it was a usual scene in a busy railway junction in India. But it melted Nivedita's heart; she felt a lump in her throat.

Suddenly, the gorgeous looking man turned to the beggar and started shouting abuses in English. He was expressing loudly his extreme annoyance at the presence of beggars near him. Nivedita, at this point, took courage and confronted the man in suit.

- Sir, you may help him or not; it is your entire wish. But please don't abuse him; the poor fellow is starving with children.
- Oh! It seems the goddess of mercy has descended on us. If you are so merciful, why can't you give that beggar some food yourself, instead of preaching others?
- Thank you, Sir. Precisely, that is what I am going to do.
- Oh! That's simply great.

The gentleman shrugged his shoulder and proceeded. Nivedita, on her part, took the beggar with the children to a food stall on the platform, bought some food for them and proceeded to the waiting train. Almost immediately, the train started.

When Nivedita was ushered in the board room where the interview was going on, she had the shock of her life. The same gentleman in suit and tie was sitting at the center of a huge table along with a few other equally distinguished looking ladies and gentlemen on his both sides. That meant he was the chairman of the interview board. She was bewildered by the turn of events and the coincidence. But the man outwardly, displayed remarkable nonchalance in his behavior. He got himself and the others introduced to Nivedita duly as if he saw Nivedita for the first time. The interview was conducted as usual. Nivedita fared well. But, he dropped the bombshell at the end:

–   My dear lady, I am afraid, you seem to be more suitable for a NGO or a charitable organization working for the poor, not for a profit oriented corporate entity like ours. I am rejecting you.

Questions:

i.   Did Nivedita do the right thing in involving herself with the beggar when she was coming for an interview?

Given her background and upbringing, she did nothing wrong in feeding a starving family. Probably, as a posterior analysis, it can be said that she should not have been as sensitive and emotional as to confront the man who was driven more by his own ego and social status rather than compassion like Nivedita. She should have silently helped the beggar without confronting anyone. These precautions in life come with age and maturity.

ii.   Did the man, in his status and situation in the station, behave correctly?

No, the man did not behave correctly. He should not have displayed his anger and annoyance on a helpless beggar publicly like that. He should have ignored and avoided the beggar silently without creating a scene and thereby drawing adverse attention. He should have controlled his temper.

iii.   Did the man do justice to Nivedita in the interview? Did he behave professionally justifying his role as a chairman of the interview board?

No, he did justice neither to Nivedita nor to the organization that hired his service and most importantly, he did injustice to his profession. He mixed up personal issue with professional issue which is unethical and improper. He deprived innocent Nivedita of a promising career, he deprived the organization that placed confidence in him and hired him of an opportunity to induct in service a good candidate like Nivedita who could be an asset to the company. Lastly, his conduct was unbecoming of a true professional.

iv.   Should Nivedita learn a lesson and change her attitude towards beggars henceforth, after this episode?

Nivedita indeed should learn a lesson but that would not be changing her attitude towards beggars. In that sense her attitude was quite alright.

She should change her approach to deal with such persons who can do immeasurable harms to her for the sake of their ego and false sense of pride. She would definitely encounter such persons in both her personal and professional life in future. She should be careful in protecting her own interest while simultaneously taking Care of helpless people according to her own conviction and upbringing.

v. Is it a HR case study at all? What HR/OB lessons you can derive from this case study?

Yes, in a way it can be called a HR case study in the sense that true professionals would not mix professional issues with personal issues. A true professional should not act or take decisions driven by a spirit of vendetta or revenge. A true professional should not destroy an innocent good candidate's future neither he should ignore the interest of the organization that hired him by misusing the platform provided to him to settle personal scores. It is an object lesson for all HR professionals engaged in recruitment and selection.

AN UNEXPECTED REWARD FOR SHOWING ENTREPRENURIAL SPIRIT

Karan Saxena, now in his late thirties, was born in an aristocratic family of Lucknow, but intriguingly, his heart was always with the grass roots i.e. people at the bottom of the pyramid. He could empathize with them strikingly, feel for their plight and be one with the downtrodden. In his childhood, when young boys in his class were joining elite cricket and football clubs in the city, he used to play those games with the slum children, he became their darling. This inclination, of course, was galling to his parents. His father was an IAS officer of UP cadre and mother was also from an affluent family in Lucknow. They were quite upset with their son's behavioral pattern and his choice of friends and associates.

His father, as a last resort, sought for a transfer to the Karnataka cadre when Karan was about to finish schools. He succeeded and got posted in Bangalore. Karan did not show any interest in the administrative service neither he was extraordinarily brilliant in his studies. He was admitted in a good local engineering college and duly passed out with a first class. He was campus selected by Asian Electronics and got posted in their main factory in Bangalore. His parents were relieved as Karan was showing signs of settling down in his own class of society. He also progressed well in his career getting regular promotions. His parents got him married with a girl, a lecturer in a local college. So, finally, in all respects, he seemed to have settled down or so his harried parents thought.

But, that was not to be as the turn of events proved subsequently. When Karan was about to touch forty, tipped for a promotion to take over a department as its head, he was struck by the so called 'middle age blues' and became very restless. He felt he was wasting his time as he was committed to greater purpose in life. That purpose also he identified i.e creating jobs and livelihood for the poor. He wanted to start a SSI, becoming an entrepreneur. His parents opposed the idea tooth and nail; surprisingly his wife supported him. There was no looking back; he went ahead and got his SSI unit registered. For capital equipments, he applied for a loan from the state financial corporation. He was interviewed by the corporation and considering his qualification and experience in industry, the loan was sanctioned with the condition that he would have to devote his full time in developing the unit. He resigned his job.

As per the condition of his appointment, he had to wait for three months to get relieved after his resignation was accepted. His employer became, of course, aghast; the company had pinned a lot of hope on his heading a profit making department and he resigned. They, however, accepted his resignation. Based on this acceptance without hassles, Karan started interviewing young boys and girls from poor families as per his conviction after taking a premise on rent. Gradually the notice period of three months was over but his release did not come by. His boss had told him to finish certain important pending work which he promptly did. Even then, his release did not come through after the expiry of two more months. Karan became impatient. The financial year was coming to an end. The term lending financial institution sent him a notice stating that the loan sanctioned to him would be forfeited if he did not avail of it within the financial year.

At this point, Karan wrote a strong representation to the management asking for his immediate release but received a charge sheet in reply. He was charged with violating the service rules by opening a private business unit without the knowledge and prior permission of the management, while during service. The financial institution also withdrew the loan accompanied by a commitment charge for not having availed the loan within the time permitted. Karan was staring at an uncertain future.

Questions:

i.   What is the meaning of the term 'middle age blues'? What is its significance in HR?

Middle age blues is a syndrome which is of extreme importance or concern for a HR manager and HR profession in general. It is encountered particularly in the white collar educated executive cadre. Mid-career executives, erudite and ambitious, mostly have one thing in common. They are less afraid of losing jobs in any particular organization because of their professional acumen and corresponding high mobility. They are more dedicated and identify themselves with a profession rather than any particular organization.

As a result, when they climb to the middle level in a hierarchy, they have a serious introspection as to how far they have come and at that rate how far they can go if they stick to the same organization. When they find that the rate of their career growth so far has been less than satisfactory and they are unlikely to fulfill their ambition by retirement, they tend to quit i.e change track. Hence, the rate of executive attrition at the middle level is very high. As they are in responsible positions, their sudden departure creates disruption in organization's functioning. It is a matter of serious concern for HR who has to evolve innovative ideas and incentives to retain them.

Sometimes, this dissatisfaction is more concerned with the line of activity and value system rather than career growth. This has been the case with Karan here. He discovered that he was pursuing a wrong value system and changed track to line of activity according to his own aspiration and value.

ii. Was there anything seriously wrong with Karan from the HR point of view? Did he display any lack of professionalism?

This question is very intriguing to say to the least and the answer is likely to be quite controversial. Let us refer to the four 'T's for the roles a HR manager plays according to Kossek and Block i.e Transaction, Translation, Transition and Transformation. Karan was not, by any means, a delinquent or undisciplined executive. Only discrepancy with him was that he was driven by different value system from the very childhood which was not approved and was suppressed by his parents. His initial conformity was due to the fact that he wanted to establish himself in life by testing the corporate water and find ground below his feet before taking the plunge. After turning an entrepreneur, it was quite unlikely that he would get any help from his parents, should such a need arise anytime in future. He, by all means, was ploughing a lonely furrow. Of course, his wife's support bolstered his confidence immensely.

But, the point is the HR functionaries in Asian Electronics either deliberately did not or could not transform him and he could not align his personal value system with those of the organization even in the long run.

iii. Was the management justified in taking Karan to task? What was the rationale behind the management's action in terms of HRM principles? It is but obvious that the management did not take Karan's entrepreneurial adventure very kindly. Management's displeasure was even more accentuated by the fact that they expected a lot from Karan as a head of a department. Even then, the management should not have been vindictive with Karan who was dedicated to his commitment in life.

HR principles do not preach or profess victimization of employees in the garb of imposing rules and regulations strictly. Management took the advantage of a gray area where an employee has resigned and his resignation has been accepted but he is yet to be released. In this intervening period, the question is whether the code of conduct should be applied strictly which turns out to be detrimental to the interest of the employee. It appears to be a calculated move to deter Karan from leaving the company.

Everything said and done, holding up Karan indefinitely without releasing him was unethical and unjust on the part of the management.

iv. What is the lesson in HRM you learn from this case study?

This case study teaches us a lot as far as the purpose of HRM is concerned. It makes us confront the question "Is HRM meant to serve the interest of the management without a reasonable regard to the interest of the employees, or vice versa, i.e is it meant to serve the interests of the employees disregarding those of the management or both? This is a classic case where the interest of one of the employees, who has been an asset to the organization so far, is directly clashing with those of the management. The most important point to be noted here Is that any forcible retention by hook or by crook, will be counterproductive in the long run i.e. if Karan is forced to stay back under adverse circumstances engineered by the management, he would not be productive as he used to be earlier.

CASE STUDY 13

INFORMATION REVOLUTION AND THE LAGGARDS

Samaresh Majumdar was pretty upset with his colleagues and sub-ordinates and started believing that they all had connived against him to let him down. They were all jealous of his success and professional progress or so he thought. In this juncture, he recollected David Mclleland's 'Achiever' which he had studied as theories of motivation during his days of management education in S.P. Jain. in Mumbai more than a decade back. He firmly believed in Mclleland's concept of an achiever. A good lot of water has flown across the Arabian Sea since then and Samaresh has almost made it or so he believed. In his mid-thirties now, he has reached the upper layer of the middle management cadre in a renowned multi product FMCG company in Mumbai. If everything was to go smoothly, he would make it to the board level or so it appeared not only to him but also to his peers. All of a sudden, the situation has turned to worse and Samaresh has been left wondering how.

About a couple of decades back, as he sometimes reminisces, he was in a desperate situation. He could not make it to a Government engineering college and private institutions were unaffordable. He had to be content with a graduate degree in pure science. But unrelenting, he studied MSc. In information technology, albeit in the distance mode and subsequently bagged a job in a small IT startup. He worked for five long grueling years and saved money resolutely from his not so fascinating salary amount. He prepared hard, sat for the entrance test and made it to S.P Jain. And the proverbial flood gate to fortune opened up for him. All these trials and tribulations over the years made him a firm believer in two things: David Mclleland and Information Technology.

During his course of service in this company his belief in these two turned into conviction. 'Achievement is not everybody's cup of tea, only a few are blessed and information is the resource of all resources, a manager is not much of a manager if he does not know how to generate and harness information.'-he used to think. Driven by this conviction, he maintained a well-guarded distance from his peers and never allowed closeness to set in and the others could sense it. He was bent upon bringing about an IT revolution of sorts in his company by introducing IT intervention in many business processes in the company.

But, unfortunately, his company could not just match up to his initiative. Though profitable since inception, it was after all a family managed concern with scant professionalism. Most of the employees were not professionally qualified and were distantly related to some member of the BoD or other. So, they were enjoying a sense of security, a sense of benign complacency as none of them was compelled to excel. Amidst this ocean of mediocrity, Samaresh was a stark exception, without a god father, driven by a thirst to excel, to outperform others without being specifically told – the hall mark of a typical Mclleland's Achiever.

All that he wanted was nothing out of the way though. He wanted a MIS installed in the company with a central server, equipped with a state of the art ERP package, custom built to automate his company's key business processes. He expressed his ideas to his boss, the divisional head, after meticulously identifying the key performance areas (KPAs). The divisional head gave him a patient hearing, was impressed, so to say, more by the initiative Samaresh took rather than the novelty of the idea. About its financial soundness, he was not too sure as ERP packages were very costly and so was a mainframe for the server. Though not a finance man, he could gauge the immensity of the financial implication of the proposal and consulted his peers from the finance department. Neither those finance men could estimate the economic value of the benefits and hence was not very enthusiastic about the idea.

Samaresh, however, did not relent. He raised the level of his appeal to the BoD, of course, with the clearance of his boss. In the absence of MIS, there was no information system directorate yet. So, he sought the attention of the operations and finance directors and asked for an appointment. The respective PAs of the directors informed him that he would have to wait for about three months to get both the directors together. He would be required to present his case in the form of a power point presentation highlighting the merits of his ideas and should be prepared to answer critical questions. Samaresh took up the challenge with the right spirit and started preparing for the presentation with the right earnest.

In the meanwhile, something sinister started happening. The news leaked out from the directors' office that Samaresh was up to something pretty ominous which might alter the work content of all the staff, middle level downwards, including even the blue collar workers. More importantly, there would be so much of initial cash outflow that the company would be bleeding for the coming five years. So far profit making, the company would incur losses, hence, there won't be any bonus in the foreseeable future. The middle level, so far basking in the comfort of security got panicky as they would be required to acquire new skills, rationalizing their whole work process to accommodate the intervention of IT in everything they do. They were neither prepared nor willing for the change at all. But, cleverly, they did not themselves flare up. They instigated the blue collar community of workers on the issue of impending loss of bonus. The trick worked, the recognized trade unions, two of them, gave strike notice jointly citing objections to the installation of MIS in the company.

Questions:

    i.   Was there anything wrong with the company at the first place?

        There were many things not exactly right. Every company, worth its name for being in the game, should have its operating core and the middle level backbone made up of professionals who are more dedicated to their profession rather than the organization, per se, managed by a family at the top. There is nothing gravely wrong if the company is owned and managed by a family at the top. Many successful Indian companies are managed thus. But, the operating core and the backbone middle level should be made up of professionals uncompromisingly. Professionalism cannot be surrendered at the altar of the exigencies of the owning family's interest. Otherwise, the interests of the other important stake holders in the publicly owned company may irreparably suffer. That was precisely the situation in this case.

ii. Was there anything right either with Samaresh, both in terms of his purpose and attitude?

As far as Samaresh was concerned, the genuineness of his purpose was unquestionable. He was a thorough professional totally dedicated to his profession, but not to the family of the owners and their cronies in the company. Had he done that, he could have secured his position in the company, but then, he would have done a huge injustice to his profession. He overlooked his own future in the company as he found and felt that his profession was being overlooked by others.

His purpose was genuine, but unfortunately, his attitude was not. As a typical David Mclelland's achiever, he isolated himself, threw public relations to the winds and paid the price for it. He should have cleverly marketed his ideas to the powers that be surreptitiously. He went ahead like a raging bull ignoring others' fears and apprehensions, which was his undoing; he became an innocent victim of others' machinations and manipulations. He should have adopted a more diplomatic approach.

iii. Was Samaresh trying to do the right thing?

Yes, by all means. His company, in today's information driven world, needed a well designed and constructed MIS really badly. The tragedy was that the top management could not grasp his idea in its entirety and was apprehensive about the financial implications. Of course, the financial issues that arise with the installation of an elaborate and functional MIS are always controversial, in any company, for that matter. The finance personnel are usually not equipped enough to quantify the benefits of the outcomes/outputs of the information system in exact financial terms and the associated time horizon for which these benefits would flow and hence this hesitation on the part of the management.

iv. Was the response of the management right to Samaresh's initiative? Should it have been different? What was lacking?

At the very first place, it was quite intriguing why an employee like Samaresh should take the initiative to get MIS installed in the interest of the company. This initiative should have been taken by the management itself, in keeping with the trend of the time. An enlightened management worth its name should be pro-active instead of being reactive as in this case. An encouraging and enthusiastic response to Samaresh's initiative on the part of the management was lacking.

Moreover, the Directors who were approached by Samaresh should have been more up and doing in maintaining secrecy about the transactions and goings on in their offices and should not have allowed their respective personal assistants to leak out vital information prematurely, which ultimately resulted in pre-empting the move and sabotage.

v.   Is there any HR issue at all, out of the main issues in this case?

Yes, of course. Irrespective of its deceptive appearance otherwise, it is indeed a classic case of HR issues. When the core competence of the company is compromised in the interest of blood relations and family loyalties, the genuine professionals with unquestionable professional commitments, who are the real assets of the company, would feel suffocated under the pressure of family loyalties all around. They will be forced to either stagnate or leave the company, which would turn out to be very harmful for the company in the long run. No HRM worth its salt can be a silent spectator to this disengagement.

vi.   What a prudent management should do under the circumstances? Should they get rid of Samaresh, the root cause of all the troubles?

Labeling Samaresh as the root cause of all the trouble would be another blunder on the part of the management. Employees like Samaresh are harbingers of constructive changes that a company has to undergo at the dictates of changing times to remain relevant in business. So, a prudent management should not only encourage but also proactively evaluate the proposal in all its ramifications as far as the company's both long and short term interests are concerned and act accordingly.

It is, by no means, recommended that Samaresh be treated or hailed as a hero neither he be condemned as a villain in the company, because both these extremes moves may be harmful for the company in one way or the other. The company cannot afford to antagonize either its blue collar work force or its intelligentsia in its own interest, so it has to tread a careful path by balancing both these opposing forces. But then, that is what prudent management is all about.

CASE STUDY 14

RETIREMENT BLUES AND INNOVATIVE HRM SOLUTIONS

Mr. Subhashish Sanyal became very emotional with tears in his eyes. He felt crestfallen and heartbroken at that very moment he has been visualizing at times during the past about a decade or so; still he was not mentally prepared to confront this inevitable moment. The fact of the matter is that he has turned sixty on 17th June this year and is due to superannuate, as per rules, on the last day of the month i.e 30th June. The farewell function has been scheduled on the day before and ''He was a jolly good fellow would rent the air'' – or so Subhashish felt. He also felt a gripping emptiness filling his life. Simply, he was not able to cope with this separation and the accompanying loss of income and loss of professional engagement and even identity. A sense of uselessness and a sense of having been discarded overtook him. His forty years of career is coming to a grinding halt and he simply did not know what to do.

Having nothing else to fall back upon, he takes refuge in memories i.e. recollection of the past as the future seems bleak and unreliable and all recollections, even of those days of hard struggles seem pleasant today. That is the charm of time which is a great healer, they say. By all means, he was an average student in school and wanted to study Commerce but his father wanted him to study Engineering. Number of engineering colleges being very limited those days, he could acquire a seat in a Poly-technique for a Diploma in Mechanical Engineering. He could find a job as a supervisor trainee in the Quality Control department of M/s. Progressive Hydraulics Ltd, an engineering industry in the MSME sector making hydraulic pumps and accessories. When he was just twenty-one, his father suddenly expired and the financial responsibility of running the whole family fell on his tender shoulders. He took his job and career very seriously as the only means of livelihood and survival.

No wonder, he, within a course of a few years, could master the intricacies of product quality aspects and became trustworthy of his seniors. His employer encouraged him to complete his graduation in mechanical engineering by sponsoring his fees and giving him leaves generously as and when he needed them to sit for the examinations and other exigencies of the evening course. As soon as he completed his graduation, he was promoted to the rank of Quality Control Engineer. But, Subhashish's thirst for academic pursuits did not end there. In course of his job, he used to have a lot of interactions with the cost accounting department functionaries who were collecting monthly rejection data to ascertain the cost of the products and he developed a fascination for cost accounting. Already he had an innate desire to study Commerce from his childhood. With the economic stability and a sense of security, this desire was rekindled. He took admission in the local chapter of the ICWA institute and the tuition.

He took about ten years to complete his Associateship in the professional institute; both he and his employer grew together during this period. His employer grew to a large-scale industry and the organization structure had to be changed to a product based one. He became an unquestionable expert in his product line and was heading his product division as a General Manager. He was totally thorough in both technical and cost aspects of his products and a pillar of professional strength for his company. When such an indispensable person was retiring, his company's management was staring at a void hard to fill in his absence. They were contemplating various possible ways and means to retain him in the company albeit without violating retirement rules.

By all means, it became a challenge for the HR department to figure out how to retain Subhashish so that the company is not deprived of his experience and wisdom together with adequately remunerating him so that he does not have to undergo any economic hardship.

Questions:

i.   What is a product based organization? What are its merits and demerits? When an organization makes multiple products of diversified kinds and each product range requires different processing, technology and management, the organization structure should be suitable or conducive for such a situation. An organization making products may start with making a single product to establish itself in the world of business and then to ensure its continuity. The corresponding organizational structure can be on conventional functional line.

When the product succeeds, the company may go for making similar products of different capacities, sizes etc. This is called a product line. As long as the company confines itself to a single product line, the functional set up may continue fruitfully. But, when the same organization for the sake of expansion and growth, embarks on a conglomerate diversification i.e. making products of different kinds and ranges, the structure of the organization should be changed to a product based one.

In a product based organization, it is decomposed into various divisions dedicated to each product line. Each division, within itself, can be structured on functional basis. If the volume of business become huge for each product line, the original company may be divided into subsidiaries catering to each product line, each subsidiary having its own Board of Directors. All these subsidiaries will come under a common holding company. This makes sense because each product line may require different expertise and different management styles and approaches and even different strategies to counter different copetitors.

The advantage of a product based organization is that services of dedicated experts are available for a particular product line; the disadvantage is cost. As the line managers are experts in a narrow area, his expertise can't be utilized in any other area. So, if the expert is not utilized fully for low capacity utilization, he would be idling. The staff people, of course, may have more interdivisional or inter-subsidiary mobility.

ii.   What is superannuation? What are its merits and demerits? Why in the developed economies all over the world, the age of superannuation is significantly higher than that in the developing countries?

When an employee retires from service mandatorily i.e. without opting for it because of reaching a particular age, this condition is called superannuation. On the other hand, when an employee takes retirement from service voluntarily by opting for it, before reaching the age of superannuation, it is called voluntary retirement. Some companies, to cut down wage bills, device incentives to induce their employees to take voluntary retirement, thereby reducing the employee strength.

In India, the standard age for superannuation of the central Government servants has been sixty years whereas still in many State Governments and the private sector it is fifty-eight years. In certain specific areas of service in the central Government, the age of superannuation is sixty-five years, for example, in academic, judicial and medical services.

The obvious benefit of superannuation is making room for fresh blood coming in i.e. old leaves have to fall off to make room for new leaves to grow, thereby solving unemployment problem to a great extent. The obvious disadvantage would be loss of experienced and matured hands to be replaced by inexperienced raw hands. In developed countries the rate of growth in capital formation is more than that of population growth. In some developed countries of western Europe, the rate of population growth is even negative. So, there is a demand – supply gap of working population and the older people can't afford to retire. Also because of advanced economic conditions and health care facilities the aging population can maintain good health and continue to work. For example, in countries like Sweden and Norway, the standard age of superannuation is seventy years.

In developing countries like India, the situation is just the reverse i.e. the rate of population growth is more than that of the economy and hence the number of vacancies created are smaller, superannuation is imposed at a younger age.

iii. Other than superannuation, what are the ways and means of separation between the employee and the employer? Enumerate and explain.

There are quite a few ways of separation between the employer and employee, other than superannuation; some of them are temporary and some permanent. They can be summarized as follows:

    a. Voluntary retirement

    b. Death

    c. Resignation

    d. Permanent/temporary disablement

    e. Termination

    f. Discharge

    g. Dismissal

    h. Lay-off/Retrenchment

    i. Lock out

    j. Strike

The first one has already been explained. The second and third do not require any explanation. The fourth one is due to medical condition caused by disease or accident. Discharge is mostly due to lack of fitness for service resulting from either physical or mental conditions. It is not a punishment and the employee being discharged gets all the separation benefits like gratuity etc. Termination and dismissal are punishments mostly on disciplinary grounds. For termination separation benefits won't be withheld but for dismissal the employee won't be eligible for any separation benefits.

Lay-off and retrenchment are both non-voluntary separation between employer and the employee at the instance of the employer. Lay off is mostly temporary whereas retrenchment is permanent. Lay-off is resorted to when there is an economic downturn and the turn over gets reduced due to myriad reasons like large scale power cut, breakdown of machinery, non-availability of raw materials, lower demand due to economic recession etc, and a part of work force are sent home for some time, to be taken back in future when situation improves. Retrenchment results in a permanent reduction in work force brought about owing to closure of a division, obsolescence of a technology or product, change in consumer behavior or test etc. Lay-off being temporary, there is no payment of gratuity involved, for retrenchment all dues are settled once for all.

The last two are also temporary separation caused by any breakage of industrial relation between employer and employees. Strikes are called/declared by the trade unions and workers do not report to work, whereas lock-outs are declared/initiated by the management as a counter measure for indiscipline, unrest, tool down etc. Both these measures involve the labour department officials of the state concerned or the central government depending upon the relevant jurisdiction.

iv. What are the ways and means for both the company and Subhashish for continued professional engagement for mutual benefit?

This would be purely a HR exercise and a few means can be contemplated. A retired person is normally no longer strong physically but mentally he can be experienced, knowledgeable, disciplined and above all, committed to both his profession and organization. These are the reasons which make him worth for a re-employment. He should be employed only on part time basis so as not to cause undue physical strain, neither he should be engaged in any executive capacity. He can be employed only in advisory or consulting capacity. His remuneration should be consolidated and appointment contractual to be renewed periodically every year. He should be required to report to a highly placed official only. His employment contract will lapse at the expiry of one-year subject to renewal or it can be discontinued/terminated by mutual consent within one year.

v. What the HR and OB lessons you derive from this case study?

A good number of lessons in HR & OB we can derived from this classic case. This case study confirms the dictum which every HR professional worth his salt believes in: Human Resources, quite unlike any other physical or material resources, is capable of unlimited development. But to bring about this, management has to ensure engagement and commitment on the part of the employees. A dedicated employee is a real asset to any organization, more such employees, stronger is the organization. Such employees should be identified at the earliest, handled cautiously and sensitively, encouraged, developed and retained at any cost.

Though it is generally believed that, in the true sense, nobody is indispensable, indeed, there do exist a few key personnel whose departure, may be for a legitimate reason, can cause untold and immeasurable harm to the interests of the employer organization. Ways and means have to be devised by the HR functionaries to retain them.

From OB point of view, we can say that when a contributing employee is identified, recognized and rewarded, it becomes an example for the other employees to follow suit and in the bargain the number of contributing employees gets multiplied resulting in the enrichment of the other stake holders.

HUMAN RETENTION MANAGEMENT

"Our strategic objective should be employee retention and that can be fulfilled by, I believe, attaining and retaining the status of a "best opportunity employer" in the industry to which we would belong." – Mr. Sundara Murthy was expressing his views and visions for the company he and his colleagues had decided to found. A group of six IITians in a reputed IT company and a mathematics lecturer from the local university have decided to turn entrepreneurs and open their new company in the IT sector. Eventually, this group of seven is, more or less, of the same age, come from the same professional area i.e. IT, except the mathematician who was Murthy's school mate. Sundara Murthy was unanimously elected to become the CEO to start with because he displayed possessing some leadership skills over and above his high technical competence and accomplishments. The group used to meet regularly at the weekends at Sundara Murthy's modest residence in the city to chalk out their future plans.

Sundara Murthy's father was a school teacher but that was no hindrance for him in nurturing his ambition i.e. to own his outfit, his own company. "If you don't have any agenda of your own, your life will be spent in fulfilling others' agenda." – was his motto. He was the inspiration behind the other six opting out of their employment to respond to his clarion call; of course, the market for business software, all over the world, especially in the US, was very fertile and lucrative. Murthy's brother –in –law, settled in the US acted as a catalyst by promising him orders for business software. Murthy's brain child "Genesis Software Solutions Ltd," saw the light of the day. In those days, company law made it mandatory to have at least seven directors to have a public limited company. But, Murthy, including himself, could gather only six. So, he had to renew his contact with his school mate, Mahesh who was well settled with the lectureship in a government institute. Mahesh did not understand software and IT but he had faith in Murthy. So, he joined.

Murthy, during his career of about eight years in a renowned IT behemoth, observed certain mismanagement and malfunctioning in handling the HR areas of his employer. The mistakes were so glaring and injustices so outright, that he took a vow, within himself, to take special pre-cautions not to repeat the same mistakes when he would have his own company. The main problem, in general, in any IT industry is employee turnover i.e. attrition. So, this particular area of HR became his prime concern. IT industry is knowledge based and knowledge belongs to people not to machines or other inanimate capital equipment. So, Human Resources is the 'Sine-Qua-Non" for an IT industry. None was more aware of this fact than Sundara Murthy himself. So, he made retention and minimum attrition his vision for his Genesis. He vowed to become the best opportunity employer in the IT industry, as a whole.

Initially, to start with when affordability was an issue, Murthy was supervising the HR function himself. As Genesis grew in leaps and bounds, it was well neigh impossible and he had to look for an expert. The head hunters hired for the purpose brought in Kaushalya Viswanathan, an IIM, Bangalore whiz kid and a renowned HR specialist. Murthy heaved a sigh of relief and concentrated on developing software and the business as the CEO. But, after a decade down the line the attrition rate was hovering around forty percent; Murthy's benchmark was twenty percent. Kaushalya, with all her expertise in HR, could not contain it and quit. The then finance man, a brilliant Chartered Accountant, Cost Accountant and Company secretary, all bundled into one, took up the mantle of this HR challenge voluntarily. Murthy had his own reservation but agreed reluctantly. But another decade down the line when Genesis has become an international giant, the employee turnover is remaining the same i.e. around forty percent. The finance cum HR genius also left in disgust. Murthy, at last, realized that his Genesis has been a financial and even operational success, but remains a glaring example of strategic failure in HR.

Questions:

i. What is a strategic objective? Fortify your answer with suitable examples for different kinds of strategic corporate objectives.

A business organization gets started by its founder/s who is/are driven by a long term vision to be realized through this organization thus set up. These visions, often having a long term perspective, are vague and lack specificity and clarity. For example, a group of people may come together and found an organization with the vision of imparting education to a section of the masses. This is a noble idea but lacks clarity in the sense that what type of education, at what level, for which section of the people etc. are not clear.

A clearer and more specific idea spelt out by a statement emerges subsequently during implementation. This is called a mission statement; for this example, the mission will specify whether it would be primary, secondary, graduation, post-graduation or research education, in which field i.e. general, engineering, medicine, law etc. and for poor, middle class or upper class. This mission enables the founders to implement their idea.

These vision and mission form a part of what is called a strategic hierarchy for the organization concerned. The next in this hierarchy is strategic objective. The strategic objective is all about the fact that every organization has a distinct identity in the world of business in terms of the product/s it makes or the services it renders and the market segment it serves. This product/service versus market scenario gives birth to strategic objective/s.

In that specific market segment, the organization has to establish its specific identity in terms of what it excels in vis-a-vis its competitors. These strategic objectives can be, for example, occupying leading position in product/service quality, best technology process, highest price, lowest price, capturing the highest market share, being the best opportunity employer etc.

In this specific case study, the founder Mr. Sundara Murthy's vision was to be known as the best opportunity employer, a pursuit in which he ultimately failed.

ii. How do you justify the belief that human resources are the most precious resource for any industry, but much more so for an IT industry?

A business organization is set up with the ultimate objective of creating wealth for its stake holders in the society at large. This wealth creation is accomplished by generating employment for the employees, by supplying/rendering products/services at an economical price to the customers, making profits and paying corporate tax to the Government, paying dividends and creating capital gains for its shareholders etc.

In this process of wealth creation, within the organization, there is continuous interaction of men, materials, machines and management in converting raw materials to finished products and delivering them to the customers. These input factors i.e. men, materials, machines and management are considered as resources for the organization to deliver the product and create customer satisfaction.

Out of these resources, materials and machines are inanimate resources and can't run themselves. Men and management are human resources responsible for utilizing the inanimate resources to create products and services. If these human resources are not properly engaged, disciplined, dedicated and committed, optimum utilization of the inanimate resources will not take Place and the efficiency and effectiveness of the organization will suffer. A company may procure the best of machines and materials but without proper utilization, the output will be inadequate and inappropriate.

Hence, there are reasons to believe that human resources are the best resources for the organization. Moreover, when we compare the respective roles of these 4-M resources in creating the output in conventional brick and mortar manufacturing organization and IT based organization, we find that the role of machines and materials in creating an IT product is minimal as IT products are knowledge products and this knowledge can't belong to an inanimate resource.

So, in IT or knowledge based industries, human resources are, by far, the best resources and will have to be retained at all cost.

iii. Why in IT industries, in general, the employee turnover, i.e. the attrition rate is traditionally very high?

The attrition rate in IT industry is traditionally very high because of the high mobility of IT professionals. The software engineers in IT industries design/engineer software or service software. Software, as a product, is an intermediate and not an ultimate product. Particularly, software for automating a staff functions i.e say finance or HRM have a lot of commonalities among different verticals and hence, software engineers are in high demand and enjoy high mobility. As human resources are the key resources in IT industry, they have to be looked after and kept motivated meticulously. They are very intelligent and sensitive to the working conditions. Once, by any chance, there is a lack of motivation and engagement, they easily tend to migrate.

Moreover, as the workforce in IT industries are not covered by the trade union acts, their grievances regarding working conditions remain unaddressed by and large and hence the high attrition rate.

iv. Is this high attrition rate a challenge for the HR functionaries alone? Is the problem HR specific or the challenge is for all the functional areas? Definitely, the high employee turnover is a challenge to the HR functionaries as motivation and employee engagements are HR issues but by no means the factors contributing to dissatisfaction, demotivation and consequent disengagement of the employees are confined within HR functional areas.

Certain policy issues like working conditions, working hours, promotions, transfers, training and development etc. are handled by the Board of Directors in a mid – sized company and HR functionaries can't be implicated. As most of the software engineers are utilized by operation people, the lion's share of the challenge lies in the operation areas. In our present case, Mr. Sundara Murthy went wrong in his judgement as he thought the issue was confined to only HR.

v. Enumerate the ways and means at the management's disposal to retain employees for any industry in general and IT industry in particular. In general, in HR parlance, it is believed that people don't change employers, they change bosses with whom they find it hard to get along. More often than otherwise, employee retention is an issue in OB rather than HR. In other words, retention is more of a behavioral issue rather than material i.e salary and promotion policy. Behaviorally there can be just two key words in retention: timely recognition and encouragement. The employer has to create a sense of confidence in the employee's psyche that none of his sincere efforts will go unrecognized and unrewarded, obviously more so in the case of IT industry.

The reason for the same is not very far to seek. IT products are direct outcomes of the software professional's own individual and collective/group efforts. A software is an outcome of the software engineer's intellect, intelligence, reasoning and disciplined effort, not a product by the machine operator, which is the case in most of the hardware products, particularly more so in these days of extensive automation.

vi. What are the HR and OB lessons you derive from this case study?

In a nutshell, the lessons in HR and OB we can derive from this case study can be summarized as: Employee retention, that too in IT industry is a real challenge. It is an extremely important issue and is too important to be left to the HR functionaries alone. Simply because whatever soothing and reassuring effect is generated by the astute HR functionaries can be successfully spoiled by the harshness of the operation professionals.

The final word is: Employee retention, that too in an IT industry is an organization wide challenge not confined to only HR and OB functional areas alone.

DAWN OF WISDOM AT THE VIRTUAL LAST MOMENT AND ITS UNWARRANTED FALL OUT

Mr. Lakshmi Narayan was growing more and more despondent and with good reasons. He was called by the Executive Director (ED) for a meeting in his office. ED, during this meeting, gave him a piece of his mind with a thorough dressing down. The inordinate delay, lack of progress in Indian Oil Corporation (IOC) project infuriated him. The customer, IOC, had given an ultimatum to the management of Asian Electronics. They would not tolerate any further hold-up or uncertainty in the development of Multi – Channel Radio Relay they had ordered for. The volume of the order, involving development and production ran into several crores of Rupees. IOC grew impatient and threatened to cancel the order and hence this reprimand. Lakshmi Narayan, General Manager and Head of the concerned division,felt humiliated after a long time in his otherwise illustrious career.

Lakshmi Narayan, during the last thirty three years of his career,has been learning several hard lessons. One of them is that he should never absorb, i.e. keep within himself any scolding received from the top; he should immediately pass it on downwards with due amplification. That is what exactly he decided to do this time. As soon as he reached his own division from the ED's office, he called a meeting with his immediate sub-ordinates, five of them, all DGMs. One grave resentment was simmering in his mind, why he alone should be crucified for the lapse of others? If credit could be distributed duly, why not discredit?

During the meeting, owing to the humiliation he had received from the higher-ups, he became emotional and lost his temper, started shouting:

– Am I the only guy receiving my salary here? Why should I take all the abuses because of your carelessness? Answer me. He thundered.

Everybody sat startled, such behaviour was quite unbecoming of him but before anybody could say anything, something drastic happened. Lakshmi Narayan's whole body started shaking. He felt a shooting pain in his chest and before anybody could realise anything, collapsed on the floor. All the five DGMs attending the meeting called an ambulance and accompanied him to the factory hospital. The attending doctor declared that he had undergone a heart attack, perhaps the first. But, it was severe. His chance of survival was very slim. He had to be kept under observation for forty eight hours before medical science could conclude anything.

But, Lakshmi Narayan, somehow survived, though he himself did not believe that he would. As soon as he regained consciousness and was able to speak, visitors were allowed and his five immediate juniors were the first to meet him in the hospital. He was a transformed man; he sounded strange:

LN – My friends, it is very nice of you to have come to see me.

DGMs: It is our duty, Sir. How are you feeling now? When you are coming back to work?

LN – That is very unlikely, my friends. I think my end is very near. I have a few regrets; I would like to share with you, now. Don't make the mistakes I made in my life.

DGMs: Why are you saying like that, Sir? We wish you come back soon; and which regrets and mistakes you are talking about, Sir?

Lakshmi Narayan paused for a while, took a deep breath and started enumerating like an obedient school child.

LN – "Firstly, I wish I had the courage to live a life true to myself, not the life others expected of me. Secondly, I wish I had not worked so hard. Thirdly, I wish I'd had the courage to express my feelings. Fourthly, I wish I had stayed in touch with my friends and lastly I wish that I had let myself be happier." He was gasping for breath; after all, he was very weak due to sickness. But, he displayed quite a bit of conviction when he spoke. He was speaking his heart out.

Everybody was spell bound, could not retort anything; they all went back with a heavy heart.

Lakshmi Narayan came back to work after about three week's stay at the hospital being declared fit to resume duty by the doctors, but management had their own designs. He was stripped of all his powers as GM of the division he was heading. A new incumbent joined in his position. His employer, being in the public sector, could not get rid of him as he was officially declared as medically fit. He was transferred to the Head Office as an 'Officer on Special Duty' (OSD). There, he was given a small table with a single chair in a small room without even a personal assistant. He had to spend his balance years of service gazing the sky, doing virtually nothing.

Questions:

i. What went exactly wrong? Did Lakshmi Narayan make any mistake in his approach?

Yes, of course. By his pious declarations, he gave an impression to the management that he could no longer be motivated. Organizational motivation by established traditional means is possible only for a so called 'rational economic man' i.e. for those who will hanker after position and possession. A business organization is driven by material objectives, not spiritual or relational i.e. for fostering good personal relationship among colleagues and sub-ordinates. Because, such pursuits may be at the cost of harming the material interests of the other stake holders.

While we are in our active career, we look for material advancements whereas when our life comes to an end and we realize it, we often regret having incurred the cost of lost relationship. It can be reasonably guessed that one of those DGMs might have reported to the higher authorities about what Lakshmi Narayan was talking while undergoing treatment in the hospital. And obviously, his utterances did not go down well with the authorities. They were worried that if Lakshmi Narayan's personal philosophy spreads around his colleagues and sub-ordinates, the company's interest will irreparably suffer.

ii. Was the ED's action correct? Could he be implicated anyway in this episode?

From HRM perspective, the ED's action was not correct. The ED in his approach and action, while conducting the meeting, should have kept in mind Lakshmi Narayan's seniority, experience and valuable contributions to the company. In HRM parlance, there is an effect termed as 'recncy effect' in which we get carried away by what happened very recently ignoring what all happened in the past.

In the current project Lakshmi Narayan was handling, there might have been lapses on his part. But that should not obliterate all his past contributions to the company. Could he head a division without having strong positive qualities? Moreover, the ED, being a senior functionary himself, should not have been harsh and rude in handling a General Manager heading a division. It appears that his meeting was counter – productive and harmful to say to the least.

iii. Was Lakshmi Narayan's regrets justified?

Yes, as has been explained earlier briefly, during our younger days, driven by ambition and motivation to achieve career success, often we neglect our relationships with colleagues, family and the society at large. We often get caught up with success mania and, in the bargain, ignore at what cost such success is achieved. We also, sometimes, forget the priorities of our lives and engage ourselves in the rat race of career advancements. When we surrender our priorities at the altar of so called success, we no longer remain ourselves.

Ironically, when we are about to breath our last i.e. in the death bed, we recollect all these sacrifices and our hearts get filled with deep regrets about what could and should have been done but was not done. By then, it would be too late to do anything about it. We can then only advise others not to repeat those mistakes.

iv. Was management's actions, after Lakshmi Narayan's recovery, justified?

This is quite a tricky question to answer: From purely humanitarian point of view, no; from corporate management point of view, yes.

From purely corporate point of view, Lakshmi Narayan's mental transformation during and after his recovery made him unfit and unsuitable for a higher management position. The immediate subordinates, the five DGMs might have taken their senior very seriously and if so, they would put their personal objectives above the corporate objectives and the organization's interest would suffer. Everything said and done, a business organization would always want its employees to make their personal interests subservient to those of the organization to serve the larger interests of the stake holders and in the bargain it remains a hard fact that a growth of career in the company would inevitably call for making certain personal sacrifices like Lakshmi Narayan made. The punitive action taken by the management reflects that concern.

On the other hand, as far as humanitarian considerations were concerned, Lakshmi Narayan was not thrown out of his job so he won't suffer monetarily. He was only stripped of his powers on account of his purported mental and attitudinal incapacity. Henceforth, up to his retirement, he would be an economic liability to the company.

v. Does this case pertain to HR or OB or both?

Sometimes, such water tight compartmentalization/categorization of a particular case may not possible as in this case. This case study gives us glimpses of both. Firstly, how inappropriately the ED behaved and their adverse consequences on Lakshmi Narayan's mental and physical health are object lessons in both HR & OB. Secondly, the punitive action management took against Lakshmi Narayan constitute a lesson in HR for us.

vi. What are the management lessons you learn from this case study?

WE can learn several lessons in HR & OB from this classic case study. A few have been highlighted in the answer to the previous question. A few more are enumerated hereunder:

i. When senior functionaries conduct progress meetings, it should be kept in mind that the purpose of the meeting is to ensure progress. The meeting should not end up in insulting and humiliating some high official and damage his self-esteem. Then, such a meeting will be counterproductive i.e doing more harm than good.

Particularly, very senior officials, like the ED, who is a member of the BoD, should be extra cautious by remembering that progress meetings are for the good of the company, not an opportunity for him to throw his weight around and offend people. Then, he will do dis-service to the company.

ii. The senior functionaries like Lakshmi Narayan should also bear in mind that a professional career is only one facet of life and there are others no less important. If progress in professional career causes damage and impairment in the other facets of life, such a progress is not worth pursuing.

iii. When big customers put pressure on the suppliers for timely supply, they indulge in doing so in their own interest without often trying to understand the ground realities and constraints prevailing in the supplier's company. A meeting should be taken as an opportunity to enlighten and apprise them of these realities and constraints so that they become more realistic in their expectations from their supplier. A customer, however big he is, must be reasonable and realistic. They should be made to understand this, albeit tactfully. The ED is the right person to have done that. He failed in his duty in this regard also.

iv. The management, as well, could have been a bit more magnanimous in handling the situation at the end i.e. while posting Lakshmi Narayan out of his home division to the head office. They should have called him and explained their stand that, in view of his fragile health condition, it won't be proper for Lakshmi Narayan to continue to head the division as before and he should do some more sedentary job. The management also should have taken some pains to identify such suitable sedentary occupation for him so that he is not made to feel ignored, left out and neglected.

v. This matter does not exactly end here. The management action to post out Lakshmi Narayan might have serious repercussions, in the sense that the five DGMs, the immediate juniors observing the entire episode may feel that whatever is happening to their boss today may happen to them tomorrow; they may get terribly demoralized. The management should take cognizance of this fact, sit with them and explain the rationale behind their action.

INDUSTRIAL STRIKE, VIOLENCE AND ITS IMPACT ON A JUNIOR EXECUTIVE TRAINEE

Ravi Prakash was elated when he received the appointment letter in his hand. His joy knew no bounds. He had been waiting for this job eagerly and with very good reasons. After his father became afflicted with paralysis and lost his earning capacity, he was the only potential earning member in the family, but his engineering degree course itself was not completed at that time. His mother was a housewife and sister had been studying in the degree college. So, the financial burden for all these three fell on his shoulders. Luckily, the family had a roof above its head, two small rooms plus an adjoining bit of a balcony, as their share in their ancestral home. Completing the degree itself was a huge struggle without any family income and meagre savings.

Those were not the days when an employer would visit the college campus, select and absorb a chunk of the graduating students. Ravi had to wander literally from door to door to land a job. Luckily, his diligence and perseverance paid off. He got selected as an 'Engineer Trainee' in a renowned Government industry in the same city i.e. for a permanent employment. The salary was not so fascinating to brag about but, at least, survival was guaranteed or so it seemed then. His aspirations and duties were about to be fulfilled i.e. looking after his ailing parents and getting his sister educated and married before he himself could settle down by acquiring a suitable life partner-nothing out of the way, anyway.

As per the appointment order, he would be an engineer trainee for a year during which he would receive a consolidated stipend. At the successful completion of the training, he would be absorbed in the regular service as an 'Assistant Engineer' in a regular pay scale. He was given a time of about three weeks to join the training. He was waiting with bated breath for these three weeks to be over. But, unfortunately, at the end of just about two weeks, all the three recognized trade unions in the industry declared strike because the collective bargaining for wage negotiations with the management failed. The management, in retaliation, declared a lock-out, sine die.

Ravi, nevertheless, with a trembling heart, approached the factory gate right on the appointed day without fail. He, however, with a few other new appointees like him, could not reach the gate. The striking workers were violent and they were picketing at the front. A few of them caught Ravi by his collar and thrashed him mercilessly. They were shouting that they were starving with their families and these new boys want to join their duties. All the boys were beaten up and none came to their rescue. A few of the new appointees were from outstation. All of them had to go back without reporting for duty.

There were more misfortunes to come. The strike continued for three long months and the management did not relent. The workers surrendered and had to go back unconditionally to join duties. However, all the new appointments were cancelled. The new appointees were construed to have joined the strikers as they failed to report for duty on the appointed day. As if that was not enough, the management issued fresh recruitment advertisement in which it was clearly written that those new appointees who failed to join duties last time could not apply again.

Questions:

i.   What is collective bargaining? Who can be the parties to it?
     Collective bargaining is a statutorily recognised and organised negotiation between the management and the recognised trade union/s regarding issues pertaining to wages, bonus and myriad other working conditions. It is often a tripartite meeting called and organized by the management as one party and involving the representatives of the trade unions and the labour department of the local Government as the others. The outcome of this process would be binding on both the management

and the workers for a specified duration of time at the expiry of which a fresh bargaining will be conducted. This is necessary for maintaining harmonious industrial relations in organized industries.

ii. Should the management have declared lock-out as retaliation for the strike called by the trade unions?

Any enlightened management should not take recourse to retaliatory measures like declaring lock out as a response to a legitimate strike called by the duly elected and recognised trade union. If the wage negotiation fails, giving a strike call is very much within the rights of the trade union and this right is guaranteed under this country's constitution.

However, if there is large scale violence, indiscipline, unrest, rioting, criminal intimidation of the non-striking work force, management may as well declare a lock out after informing and consulting with the representatives of the local/state government.

From the brief narration of this case, it appears that the conditions were indeed compelling for the management to declare a lock out.

iii. Do you think what the management did to the new trainees was right? How the management should have handled the situation?

The way management treated the new trainees was not at all right. It is certain that the management abdicated its responsibilities toward the new trainees in ensuring their safety and safe guarding their interests. The management was well aware of the date of joining given to new comers and hence, it should have taken help from the local police force and its own security to ensure a safe passage for the new comers to join. They were totally innocent and some of them were even from outstation totally unaware of the local conditions of unrest. They became innocent victims of the management's blunder. This blunder was further compounded by the subsequent vindictive attitude of the management as they barred these innocent victims' entry in the next batch, thereby jeopardising their livelihood.

It can be, at this juncture, advised that these new trainees, who have suffered due to the management's indiscretion, can form an association and take recourse to a legal action; they have a high chance to succeed.

iv. What are the lessons in industrial relations/HRM you learn from this case study?

There are a few bitter lessons to learn from this case study:

a. Once appointment letters are issued it is but expected that so many new appointees would join as it was a question of their survival. It becomes the bounden duty of the management to create conditions to ensure safety and security of those new appointees under any adverse circumstances. In this regard, management squarely failed in discharging its duties and fulfilling its responsibilities.

b. Any management worth its salt should make it a point to ensure continuity of harmonious industrial relations in the interest of all the stake holders including the government. If the production comes to a standstill, everybody suffers; there is no gainer in this game. Management should avoid any breakage of industrial relation at all costs.

c. The workers and their trade unions, being in the level they are, will always see their own interests ignoring the interests of all other stake holders and call a strike if they are not happy. But, the management should be magnanimous enough to look at the issue in a larger perspective i.e. take corrective steps to ensure and safeguard the interest of all the stake holders. That is the essence of good corporate governance. The management, under these adverse circumstances should always take recourse to a balancing act so that pampering, promoting or safeguarding the interest of one class of stake holders should not adversely affect the interests of any other class of stake holders. Here the management action was harmful for all the stake holders.

d. Management, under any circumstances, should not be vindictive or revengeful to any class of workers, that too to the innocent new appointees. The presumption that the new appointees joined the strikers and deliberately did not join duty was outrageous and misleading. By all means, the new appointees should have been given opportunity to join as soon as the factory was opened at the end of the strike.

CASE STUDY 18

STRATEGIC RECRUITMENT BLUES

The time was around the turn of the present century, or should we say the millennium? It was around December 1999. Mr. Ranjan Majumdar, in his early fifties, General Manager and Head of the Radar division of M/s. Hindusthan Electronics, Bangalore felt pretty excited and thrilled that day. An alumnus of the oldest IIT and a recognized expert in radar signal processing, Ranjan was basking in the glory of his own, his team and of course, his company. The Meteorological Radar that his team had designed and offered got accepted by the customer i.e. the Met Department, Government of India. The occasion called for nothing short of a celebration and quite rightly, the management was throwing a party involving his division and the customer's representatives at the officers' club. Of course, Ranjan would play the host on behalf of his employer.

The party, as expected, went off very well, but while driving home back, Ranjan felt uneasiness and congestion in his chest. He went to bed straightaway after changing dresses, but could not sleep. At around 4–30 AM, he could not breath anymore and collapsed. His wife and children, with the help of neighbours, took him to the nearest nursing home. They declared him 'brought dead,' the death being due to a sudden cardiac arrest.

Yes, it was a tragedy, a disaster not only for Ranjan's family, his aged and ailing mother, but also for his division. The sudden vacuum had to be filled up at the earliest as a lucrative order was expected from the Met department which would have to be delivered by the crucial due date.

Ranjan had the requisite expertise and finding a suitable replacement was a tremendous challenge for the management. Ranjan had five Deputy General Managers (DGMs) as his immediate sub-ordinates. But the challenge lay in the fact that all the five were contemporaries i.e. of the same age groups (around 50), same qualification (B-Tech) and the same length of service i.e. twenty five years hence, promoting any one of them would almost certainly mean the end of the road for the others.

Their experience, exposure and expertise were confined within a narrow and niche area of technology and transferring any one of them to any other division that too at the helm, would be counterproductive as the expertise needed by any other division would be different. The top management was quite aware of these issues and for the first time in the history of the company as a marked departure from established practice, the company decided to bring in an expert from outside as a General Manager. Intense head hunting was embarked upon, mostly in other public sector enterprises under the same ministry having similar line of business.

The talent search yielded result within a couple of weeks and Shri Ganesh Acharya, an alumnus of NIT, Surathkal and working in the Electronics division of HAL, Hyderabad, was identified. Ganesh was already a GM, in his early fifties, wished to settle in Bangalore before retirement. It was a God sent opportunity for him more for social and family point of view rather than professional.

In the meanwhile, an order for 137 Met radars, running into hundreds of crores of Rupees materialized soon after. That was about the good things; the fall-out of this appointment or the downside was also very severe. All the five existing DGMs put in their papers, seeking voluntary retirement. As if that was not enough, all the twelve Managers next in the hierarchy started non co-operation with the newly appointed GM. No purchase order for material procurement was being processed and it was taking about six to nine months for the ordered material to land as very many of them were imported.

Acharya realised it was not his cup of tea and saw imminent failure staring at the face. He approached the Director, Operations i.e. his immediate boss and apprised him of the grim situation. The Director, in turn, called an emergency meeting of the Board. The Board entrusted the job on the Director, Commercial to convince the customer to give more time. Met department did not budge, insisted on execution of the order on time. As a way out, the BoD of Hindusthan Electronics decided to resort to outsourcing.

Ganesh Acharya, the man Friday, was again summoned by the Board to broker a deal with the HAL, Hyderabad, using his good offices to execute the order. The order amount will be an addition to HAL's turnover; Hindusthan Electronics would get a commission on profit which was pegged at 12.50% of the total cost of production. Ganesh took it as a challenge to prove his worth to his new employer and succeeded in his diplomacy. The order was delivered on time as HAL rose to the occasion. Hindusthan Electronics had to be content with the commission only.

Questions:

i. Was there anything seriously wrong with Hindusthan's promotion policy

There were shortcomings which are usually there in most of the public sector undertakings of the Government, either state or central. But this usual shortcoming became very serious due to circumstances i.e. the sudden death of a senior functionary. The death brought about a crisis situation.

Even otherwise, there was lack of wisdom and farsightedness on the part of the HR functionaries. To have five DGMs with the same back ground and seniority in a single project is a sure shot prescription for heartburns which can arise anytime to come. Five DGMs should not have been deployed in a single project; they should have been dispersed to different projects much earlier i.e. much before their promotion was due.

Moreover, bringing a new incumbent in a senior position is always fraught with problems, in any organization for that matter. The most obvious and well known solution to avert such a situation of bringing in a senior incumbent from outside is 'grooming' which is practised widely in many organizations whether private or public. It consists of identifying an internal functionary with leadership qualities in the hierarchy and grooming him up to take over as and when the need arises, whether due to regular retirement, resignation or death. Thereby, the company can avoid what is called a leadership vacuum so that it does not have to fall back upon bringing a new incumbent from outside.

ii. Does the main issue raised in this case study pertain to HR or some other functional area of management?

By and large, it is a HR case study as it involves separation due to sudden death and how the consequent vacancy was filled and the problems and challenges associated with that. But it has also elements of Operation and Strategic management in the sense that conducting a project successfully and securing the approval of the professional customer are operational issues.

When the project ran into the rough weather, the line of action the BoD opted for, subsequent negotiation with some other organization that resulted in a timely and successful delivery are issues pertaining to strategic management.

iii. Had you been a member of Hindusthan's BoD, would you have managed the situation differently? How?

Yes, had I been in such a vantage position, I would have done something a bit different as follows:

a. I would have introduced organization wide succession planning and grooming much beforehand so that crises in such exigencies are avoided.

b. I would have sat with those five DGMs for counselling before bringing in an outsider. I would have explained to them, albeit confidentially, how it was inevitable to bring in an outsider who was equally qualified, experienced and similarly placed in a similar professional organization and how his professional association would help the company to tide over the situation.

In the same counselling session, I would have also emphasised on the point that they should have a bit of conscience and a sense of gratitude to their mother organization that has nourished them for so many years and that they should not leave it high and dry in a crisis situation brought about by purely exigencies of circumstances.

They should have been loyal to their profession, at least, if not to the organization. Shirking responsibility in that critical juncture would go against professional ethics.

c. During negotiation with HAL, I would have seen to it that the whole turnover be not given to them lock, stock and barrel. I would have insisted on retaining a part of the process with us and outsourced more difficult part at a negotiated cost. Had HAL not agreed to the proposal at the outset, I would have taken recourse to hard lobbying in the ministry to bring pressure on HAL to agree.

iv. As a keen student of management, what lessons you derive from this case study?

The answer to this question will, by and large, be the sum and substance of the answers given in the previous three questions and a repetition is uncalled for. A few minor points may be added:

a. In designing the performance evaluation check list/pro forma, an item of evaluation should find a place. This would be particularly for middle and senior level executives. It would be about how the executive concerned co-operates with the management during a challenging situation or crisis. It should also be about how much the executive abides by his professional ethics irrespective of difficult or trying situations.

v. Do you think maintaining executive health is an issue here? What are your recommendations?

Yes, indeed, it is very much an issue in this case. All the executives should be thoroughly counselled by the company's doctors regarding what is professional stress, how not to become a victim of that and hoe to maintain good health in the interests of the company, family and self. There should be extensive training sessions in Yoga conducted by specialists engaged for that from outside.

TRAINING AND DEVELOPMENT BLUES

Asian Avionics has been a gem of a high tech electronic industry situated at the outskirts of Hyderabad, the city which shelters a number of defense laboratories under DRDO. In fact, it had been set up by a group of ex-DRDO scientists whose vision was to create an ideal organization oriented mainly towards employee welfare so that the company could be one of the best opportunity employers. But, they were all scientists, they needed a HR expert. After a good deal of head hunting, they zeroed on Neeraj Saxena, an alumnus of XLRI, Jamshedpur who felt lost and unrecognized in a large organization he had been working for. He was looking for a medium sized company where he could head the HR function and he found Asian Avionics or rather, they found each other.

Neeraj Saxena's professional wisdom was telling him that the most disgruntled class of employees in a high – tech company like Asian Avionics would be those who were not that professionally highly qualified but committed and good at work, enriched by experience. This class of employees are often talented, competent, intelligent, dedicated but owing to some adverse family circumstances could not pursue their higher professional studies. In their corporate career they do all the bull work but rarely get due recognition and promotion they deserve due to lack of qualification. Nevertheless, they can be developed immensely by meticulously designed training programs. They can not only match their qualified counterpart, they can even surpass and in the process, their commitment to the organization also can be secured, because it is the professional training imparted by the company is the main reason for their growth.

Driven by this conviction, Saxena designed a three – week training program to the best of his ability. He also identified and contacted the expert professional trainers, received the quotes from them and prepared the budget for the program incorporating the trainers' charges and also the charges for twenty days in an upper-mid segment hotel in Hyderabad. The total budget amount for the entire program targeted to cover about two dozen employees came to quite a substantial amount. He prepared a file giving the names of the trainee employees, the trainers, the hotel, the budgeted amount and sent it to the management for approval.

His proposal was turned down. The scientists manning the Board of Directors felt that there was no advantage in either hiring outside experts or an expensive hotel, rather the program for their own employees could, as well, be held in the factory itself and it could be imparted by a few identified and qualified engineers at the middle level of the company as the proposed training was purely company specific and no outside expert would have clear idea about the company's products and services. They called Saxena and advised him:

i. Locate a suitable hall in the factory to accommodate about thirty people and equip it with the latest requisite facilities to serve as a permanent training venue for the company

ii. The BoD itself identified three blue eyed and promising engineer-MBAs who were at the middle level to deliver the program

Eventually, the trainees, by and large, also belonged to the mid-segment who were finding their further way upward blocked. They were all middle aged but the trainers all younger postgraduates.

Saxena, though not fully convinced, did his ground work well. He sat with the trainers and chalked out a detailed half day, forty session program. He got the hall furnished with the most modern equipments and facilities within the budgeted amount and time. He also arranged for morning breakfast, coffee, lunch and even tea for the entire contingent for twenty days. The training program was announced with great fanfare in which the CMD himself took the initiative. But, most surprisingly, a good number of people in the target audience started applying for leave of any hue during the proposed period of training. Quite a few of them also reported that their granny fell seriously sick and had to be hospitalized. The training program never took off due to the lack of co-operation from the participants. Saxena felt terribly dis-appointed.

Questions:

i. Was Saxena's targeting the class of trainees correct?

Yes, Saxena's wisdom served him correct. In high tech organizations, qualification particularly technical qualifications are highly, sometimes unduly, valued. There will be almost invariably, a class of employees who are intelligent and gifted but due to some quirk of fate or lack of support from the family at an early age, could not either undertake or complete their engineering graduation. A few of them may be diploma holders in engineering and they find employment in the supervisory cadre to start with, at a young age. They gradually but patiently work their way up in the ladder.

They lack mobility and hence are loyal to their employer and concentrate on their job sincerely. They are invaluable assets to their employer. But, they find their way further up blocked due to qualification bar. They get stagnated and frustrated.

So, to continue to remain assets to the company, they need extensive training and development for re-motivation and also to get the confidence that their company still cares for them.

ii. Was his own initial plan correct?

Yes, prima-facie, it appears to be correct. The crux of the issue is that the trainees should be given experience totally different from their day to day mundane experience in their regular work and the workplace. They should also be given the impression that their employer is spending a lot of money for them and hence they are very important for the company. This psychological morale boost is the essence in motivating them rather than the actual technical material content of the training.

The crux of the issue was not only the training program which was but half of the story. Saxena, to make the training program more acceptable, should have complemented the program with a career development plan for the trainees who could successfully and sincerely take and complete the training. Basically, stagnating employees would be more interested in their career growth rather than a training program, per se.

iii. Was the modified plan proposed by the BoD correct?

Well, it does not quite seem to be. Saxena's original plan was changed mainly for the sake of economy, i.e. to cut the cost but in the bargain the whole appeal for the program was sacrificed. This is the essence of HRM in general and Training and Development in particular. The employees' psyche is something really worth exploring.

As has been hinted earlier, employees, during their training, for it to be appealing, need a novel experience delivered in a novel surrounding and that too delivered by people of novelty, not by those they meet regularly in course of their work. Post graduate engineers, about twenty years' younger and working with them, will not be accepted as trainers, however brilliant they are. While cutting costs, these vital points the BoD ignored with its consequent inevitable fall out.

iv. What went wrong exactly?

We can summarize these following flaws in the program design:

a. The training program was not backed up by a reward i.e. career growth program.

b. The venue of the training program lacked novelty.

c. The program was planned to be delivered by people much younger in age with less experience

d. The program was planned to be delivered by people who were too familiar to the trainees and familiarity breeds contempt.

e. The entire planning betrayed the intention of cost cutting by the management which the trainees did not like.

v. What lesson in HR you learn from this case study?

A keen student of HRM has a scope to learn a lot from this simple looking but actually not so simple case study. Firstly, it appears by reading the narration in between the lines that Saxena wanted to prove his worth and create a favourable impression for himself in the company by doing something quite novel to start his career as the Head,

HR functions. His forte might have been training and development and he targeted that area to start with. He also successfully identified the most dissatisfied but productive group of employees in the company and according to his judgement, that particular group needed training the most. So far, everything seems to be in place.

But, Saxena made mistakes immediately afterwards. He should have first introduced and implemented training and development as a companywide measure and as a policy issue, meant for all classes of employees not only a focused target class. This focusing made it obvious that there was something wrong with this particular group so they only needed training and others were alright. But, in reality, all classes of employees need training of one type or the other. This targeting made the group sensitive of their own shortcoming. As a retaliatory measure, they started finding shortcomings in the training design and ultimately boycotted it, en masse.

Saxena should have convinced the BoD to adopt training and development as a policy and upon approval, should have designed program for each class and announced the whole plan together for everybody. That would have made his plan more acceptable.

The other shortcomings have already been highlighted and don't need repetition. As a summary, the ultimate lesson that we should learn is that any welfare measure, however good intentioned, may backfire because of unwise implementation. After all, HRM is all about handling human beings who are, at times, very sensitive and touchy.

CASE STUDY 20

DIVERGENT DESTINIES AND IRONIES OF CORPORATE LIFE

Strange are the ways the destiny of human beings takes its course, at least, that was how it seemed to Parameshwar Gogoi who was pondering over the fate of his close friend, Pratul Bora. Both of them are from Guwahati, the capital city of Assam and they studied together their graduation and post – graduation. Graduation from Guwahati engineering college, Parameshwar was from electronics branch and Pratul from mechanical. After graduation, the two went for post-graduation in the nearest IIT at Kharagpur. In those days, IIT Guwahati did not come into existence. Both of them, simultaneously, got recruited and inducted in Asian Electronics, Bangalore, through campus recruitment and landed in Bangalore and they were lodged in the trainee engineers' hostel.

In fact, just at that moment when parameshwar was travelling down the memory lane, he was sitting in a bus from the railway station to his residence at night when this thought overwhelmed him. He went to the city railway station to see off his friend Pratul Bora who boarded the Bangalore-Guwahati Express, deciding to leave Bangalore for ever after three years of stay in the southern city. Bangalore has been anything but kind to his friend-Gogoi was thinking. Both were trying their best to cope with the southern culture to which they were exposed all of a sudden. Parameshwar was posted into the R & D division by virtue of his post graduate qualification from a premier institution and hence had to deal with mostly engineers like him. The lingua-franca of the department was English and he had no problem in interacting with the locals. But Pratul was not so lucky; he specialized in production systems and got posting into the machine shop mostly populated by the blue-collar machinists. The important problem was, of course, communication. Pratul was somehow managing through his supervisor, a local, who could manage English to some extent. Both Parameshwar and Pratul got their services confirmed in the post of Deputy Engineer after completing their mandatory service period of one year as probationers.

Two more years passed and their first promotion in the hierarchy i.e. to the post of Senior Engineer became due and both hoped to get it as a matter of course. Both of them were contemplating to settle down in the costly IT capital of India, until one day something drastic happened to Pratul as fate intervened.

On that fateful day, Pratul's duty commenced at sharp 6:30 AM on the machine shop floor and he was the in-charge. While taking a stroll across the shop floor, he found machine No 7 idle and unattended. Flabbergasted, he called the supervisor. It was the habitual offender Govinda, the machinist concerned who did not report for duty yet. Govinda was a rogue, highly undisciplined and unmanageable. Pratul got depressed and went back to his chamber.

Immediately after the morning tea break, Govinda showed up and it was clear from his conduct that he was drunk. He was in a hurry, as if to make up for the delay. As he loaded the machine, the tool broke and the job was damaged, sure to be rejected. The material damaged was very costly and scarce. The supervisor came running and started scolding Govinda. Govinda, in retaliation, caught the supervisor by his collar and started hitting him shouting abuses. Hearing the pandemonium, Pratul came out of his chamber and separated the two. Now, Govinda started hitting Pratul and startled, the other workers rushed in and intervened.

Pratul reported the matter to the higher-ups and Govinda was suspended, pending enquiry, summarily. But, within about a week, he was back. The trade union took up Govinda's case and prevailed upon the management by convincing them that it was actually Pratul's fault. Govinda turned a drunkard under undue pressure created by Pratul's rough handling and prolonged misbehavior. And, surprisingly, the concerned supervisor also, when questioned, kind of supported the view propagated by the trade union. As the supervisor was an eye witness, his deposition carried weight and it was then the turn of Pratul to get the wrong end of the stick. He was suspended and for him there was no union to defend him. He lost not only his promotion but also an increment.

That was enough for Pratul and he put in his papers.

Questions:

    i. Who was actually at fault, Pratul, the supervisor, Govinda, the trade union or the management?

        Out of all the parties or stakeholders mentioned in this episode, only Pratul was the loser as an innocent victim. All the others were at fault. The hero of this episode was, of course, Govinda with all his indiscipline, lack of character and his wayward behavior. All the other entities played supporting roles in covering up the misdeed. The supervisor falsified under pressure from the trade union. The trade union flexed its muscle to demonstrate how they can protect their member under any circumstances by influencing the eye witness. The management on its part was inept and spineless. The net result was the sacrificial goat named Pratul Bora hailing from a distant land.

    ii. What could be the real reason for Govinda's mis-behavior?

        It is difficult to point out the exact cause of Govinda's misbehavior, but one thing seems certain. In most of the manufacturing industries, that too in the central public sectors like Asian Electronics, the blue-collar workers are locals speaking the local language, not familiar with English or any other Indian language. So, they can be chastised only in their own mother tongue. Use of any other language will be ineffective. That was the problem with Pratul, he was not familiar with the local language and culture and Govinda took advantage of that.

        Moreover, it is but human nature that when there is laxity in supervision, strong support from the trade unions to cover up misdeeds, the working class will be but undisciplined. It is an inherent problem with the system, innocent engineers like Pratul hailing from far off places will only be the victims of such a faulty system.

        In deeper analysis, however, we may have a different perspective. Govinda's personal, family or social life might have been intensely unhappy owing to which he might have turned alcoholic and under the influence of alcohol, he may not be in a position to control his own behavior despite his best intention. The narration of the case does not highlight this issue. But, such a possibility can't be ruled out.

iii. Why the supervisor, in reality, did not categorically support Pratul by testifying against Govinda during the enquiry by the management? What could be the real reason?

The answer to this question has been hinted in the answers to earlier questions. There can be several valid reasons for such a partial, dishonest and illogical behavior on the part of the supervisor such as:

a. Firstly, the supervisor's partiality in favor of a fellow co-worker might be out of a deep-rooted parochialism. Both the supervisor and the worker concerned might be from the same local community and language group whereas the engineer was from a different distant land and might have been considered as an outsider. When there is a conflict between a local and an outsider, sympathy from a local will be for the local not the outsider, however unreasonable and misplaced that sympathy might be.

b. From a generic point of view, it can be said that a supervisor joins any organization as a blue-collar worker first. He is not a supervisor from the day one but becomes one after showing some merit, but attitudinally continues to belong to the working class, not the educated executive class. During any conflict between the two classes, he takes the side of the working class.

c. When the management is not visibly or conspicuously strong enough, any supervisor, for that matter, will be afraid of taking side of the executive class fearing retribution from the working class and will hesitate to testify against it.

d. The last bit not the least, the supervisor testified against the executive more out of fear rather than dictates of his own conscience. The executive community, anywhere, is not united and if one of this community is harmed, however unreasonably, the community can't retaliate more by design rather than default. Hence, there was no point in supporting an executive who could neither reward nor reprimand. An executive is vulnerable like a toothless tiger.

iv. What lesson you derive from this case as a student of HRM?

A keen student of management can derive a number of bitter lessons from this case study:

a. This case provides a typical instance of malfunctioning of management in general and HRM function in particular. This case highlights how a management can be spinelessly sold out to the vicissitudes and machinations of trade unions and undisciplined working class by making a sacrificial goat of an innocent executive who can't retaliate as a class.

b. This case also teaches us about the ineptness and inefficacies of organized enquiries conducted by management with a good deal of fanfare and publicity. The findings may be anything but the truth and an innocent may suffer in the bargain. The enquiry worth its name should be objective and dedicated to finding the facts not being swept by popular sentiments.

c. The management has given in by surrendering itself to a powerful lobby and finding the easiest way out but thereby threw professional ethics to the wind in the exigencies of circumstances.

d. No true HRM professional, dedicated to the profession and its ethics should be a privy to such a blunder. Here professionalism was the first casualty not the executive, per se.

e. This case in not only about crime by one and punishment to another. It has got other constructive dimensions worth noting. When a pan India organization recruits its executives from all over India, during the probation period before posting, these trainees should undergo training to gain familiarity with the local language and culture. HRM has to organize this.

f. Engineer trainees converging to Bangalore from all over India should be lodged in the trainees' hostel during the probation period before posting. That arrangement will immensely facilitate not only their knowing each other but also overcoming initial shock due to the difference in food habits, culture, language and practices etc.

CASE STUDY 21

PARTICIPATING IN THE SPACE MISSION AND THE BECKONING DEPTH OF THE LAKE

Sandeep Goel was relaxing in his easy chair on the balcony of his two-bed room apartment in Green park, a posh area in New Delhi. He was in his mid-sixties and cultivated the practice to often allow his mind to travel down the memory lane. His two grown up sons had settled down in the US and he had nothing to worry about. Originally hailing from Saharanpur in UP bordering Punjab, his father, a diploma holder in electrical engineering those days, found employment in the DoT in Delhi under the central government and had settled down in the capital since then. His father bought this apartment and Sandeep inherited it as his only son, he did not have to do anything. Apart from his handsome pension, Sandeep accumulated enough savings for his and his wife's future. He was, sort of, detached from his sons who kept contact over phone only during festivals. Otherwise, there was not much of interaction.

Sandeep, though a northerner, spent the later part of his student life and the whole of his working life in southern India. After finishing his CBSE plus two in a Kendriya Vidyalaya in Delhi, he moved to the REC, Trichy (now NIT), the best of the RECs even today, by bagging a merit seat in BE, Electronics. After graduation, he moved to Bangalore, finding employment in Asian Electronics. He lived in Bangalore up to his retirement at sixty and then moved to Delhi, as if, only to occupy the flat lying vacant after his widowed mother's death; renting it out seemed too risky. Forty years or so was not a small duration and over these years, he became very fond of and familiar with the southern hues and splendor, mainly culture. As he developed a virtually unbreakable attachment with the south, of late, he started undergoing bouts of nostalgia remembering many occasions and events, some pleasant, some not so pleasant and some even tragic.

One such a tragic incident that has started invading his mind, of late, was about Jose Verghese and the others in his team of radio mechanics and fitters who were working in his team in a challenging project during the mid-eighties when Sandeep was just a Deputy Manager heading a team of equipment developers catering to ISRO. The time was around July, 1986 and ISRO was gearing up for their ASLV project. VSSC, Trivandrum, had placed a handsome order covering a good number of mission critical and costly flight packages to be manufactured within a short period and at a short notice. Sandeep's employer, Asian Electronics, took up the challenge and Sandeep was entrusted with the job. It was such an emergency and time was so short that the whole team had to work day and night to complete the work.

Jose Verghese, hailing from Kottayam district of Kerala, was the chief radio mechanic and the Senior Technical Assistant for the whole team. His name was suggested by Sandeep himself because he thought a man from Kerala would be in a better position to interact with a customer from Kerala and he was not wrong. Upon recommendation from Sandeep, Jose received advanced training at VSSC, Trivandrum for space grade work. There was no other fully qualified engineer than Sandeep and the work demanded an extremely high level of skill in electronics and mechanical engineering due to the stringent quality norms in space. The whole team rose to the occasion, worked in unison, met the challenge and finished making all the units well within the dead line. During this untiring effort, Jose's dedication, commitment and organizing skill in ensuring everybody's co-operation was really exemplary. Sandeep got all the credits and accolades but Sandeep's conscience was pricking, he acknowledged, albeit within himself, that it was all due to Jose.

The very next step posed a different challenge of transportation. The entire consignment needed to be packed as per standard and transported to Trivandrum for the customers' inward inspection. Carrying by passenger aircraft was ruled out firstly as blue – collar workers were not allowed to travel by air and secondly, the luggage charges would be prohibitive. Bus travel was also ruled out as the consignment was too bulky and delicate to withstand the jerks. Only alternative was by rail and only one train was running those days connecting Bangalore with Trivandrum i.e. the Island Express which was completely full for several days to come. It was the desire of all involved to see that the equipment, the final and concrete result of their blood and sweat, would find a place in the space, the ultimate destination. They felt rightfully proud to have contributed their mite to India's prestigious space venture.

But, perhaps, God willed otherwise or so it appears now. Asian Electronics, being a government concern, put pressure on railways to get emergency quota released for three workers. Sandeep did not want to part company with his dear colleagues and the consignment and wanted to travel with the team. But his bosses saw red; Sandeep was in the middle management cadre, was not allowed to travel with the blue-collar workers as a matter of company policy. In the view of the management, maintaining a respectable distance was necessary even in the exigencies of circumstances and in this instance, it was not essential. Sandeep was asked to travel by air a day or two before his colleagues' departure and set the ground ready with the requisite test instruments so that the inspection/evaluation could commence with the right earnest as soon as the consignment arrived.

Sandeep felt an intense discomfort with the arrangement within himself but fell in line. Lastly, he requested his boss to allow him to carry in his briefcase a few light weight flight packages so that some progress could be made in the meanwhile. His boss reluctantly agreed. Paperwork had to be repeated for excise duty exemption. Sandeep's flight was at 9:30 AM, the train was at 9:30 PM the same evening. It was a matter of a gap of only twenty-four hours to reach Trivandrum, Sandeep thought. Upon reaching Trivandrum, after lunch, Sandeep, with the help of VSSC engineers involved, rigged up the test set up and started offering the packages he carried. By the next day lunch time, the packages got through. Sandeep felt assured within himself that, at least, a few of his handiwork would see the light of the day in space. Then, it was a patient wait for the main consignment and his colleagues to arrive, which, however, they never did. Island Express was scheduled to reach Trivandrum by 2:30 PM Sandeep waited up to 5:30 PM, nothing happened.

At the end of the day, Sandeep was called by the divisional head in his office at the ninth floor. Reaching his office, as the PA ushered him in, he found five other divisional heads present there. But, all of them put on sad countenances, as if some great tragedy had befallen and so it was. The divisional head concerned with Sandeep announced "Sandeep, I am deeply sorry to inform you that today's island express coming to Trivandrum has derailed and plunged into the 'Ashtomoody Lake' around 12:30 PM near Quilon and the bogey in which your colleagues were coming here is deep inside water. I am afraid none of them may be alive." Sandeep felt a thunder bolt from the sky above had struck his head and he slumped into an empty chair. Sandeep never saw Jose Verghese and his two other colleagues again; the consignment also could not be traced from the bottom of the lake.

Subsequently, Sandeep was asked to remake those electronic devices quickly so as to avoid ISRO's program getting affected. He was given new colleagues to work with. But, unfortunately, he could not do anything as he suffered from severe 'Projectitis' and ISRO had to look for another vendor.

Questions:

   i. Was the management right in recognizing only Sandeep's effort?

     Not at all. Any success of a project is a positive outcome of all the participants' efforts. The management resorted to a shortcut and recognized only Sandeep because he was heading the team. But, contribution was made by everybody involved. Let us not lose sight of the fact that if any member of the team fails to do his part, the project would remain incomplete. As Sandeep was in the managerial cadre, he hogged all the limelight and that was unjust. Unfortunately, many project management organizations suffer from this malady.

  ii. Was Sandeep's team formation right? What could be a better team and why?

     No. When we read the narration of the case between the lines, we find that Sandeep's team formation was faulty and incomplete. Sandeep was the only officer in the team, that too, at the middle level. The immediate junior was a supervisor i.e. Jose Verghese and the others were plain blue – collar workers. There was a vacuum in the absence of a junior or lower level officer. For any important project there should be a next level of command i.e. a successor so that in any eventuality, if the head of the team becomes dysfunctional, the sub-ordinate officer can take over, albeit temporarily and the project should not suffer.

That was what exactly happened in this case. Sandeep could not function after the accident due to mental shock and projectitis and there was no immediate junior to take over and as a result the whole contract was lost. There should have been an immediate junior officer whom Sandeep could have trained up.

iii. Was the management right in not allowing all the members to travel together? What are the pros and cons of the arrangement the management made?

Yes, it appears that the management was more right than wrong for having taken this measure. The structure of a business organization meant for wealth creation is a power structure not exactly based on friendship and fellow feeling. They are, after all, informal developments which may or may not favor the formal structure, depending on situation.

Here, of course, as a post-facto analysis, we can say with all certainty that had management allowed the whole team including Sandeep to travel together by train, all would have perished and nothing would have reached ISRO at all. But, definitely, management was not aware of such an eventuality beforehand.

In this regard, management's judgement was based on the dictum that Sandeep, particularly when on an assignment outstation, should have been in total command and development of any kind of brotherhood and bonhomie would have come on the way of his having total control. That is the justification of this decision taken by the management.

On the con side, it can be said that human relations, even in a formal organization structure is very important as was established by Elton Mayo in his Hawthorne experiment in the Western Electric Company, USA. Any formal structure of command and control should not be bereft or devoid of compassion and empathy among the workforce, provided of course, such sentiments are directed productively.

iv. What is 'projectitis' mentioned in this case? How was Sandeep suffering from that?

Projectitis is a psychological phenomenon relevant particularly in project management. In a project, the human resources work together for a limited duration of the project as contrasted with production where the human resources work together for a longer duration of indefinite continuity. As projects involve intense activity for a shorter duration, a lot of attachment develops among the workforce and when one fine day, the project gets over and the team is dismantled, people undergo a psychological shock of a sudden separation from one another.

When one project gets over, the people working in it get distributed among the various other projects undertaken subsequently but they suffer from nostalgia remembering the good old days of the past association and, hence, can't concentrate on the present assignment at hand. The present project suffers thereby posing a challenge to the managers of the present project.

From this foregoing discussion, it should be clear why Sandeep was suffering from severe projectitis that eventually paralyzed him. Had the separation from his erstwhile colleagues happened naturally i.e. at the completion of the project, the shock would not have been so severe. But the separation was totally unexpected and due to a tragic accident, he could not cope with the shock.

v. Is it, after all, a HR case study at all? What are the HR issues involved?

Yes, indeed, it is a case pertaining to HRM particularly in project management. The issues involved are:

 a. A faulty project team formation.

 b. Recognizing only Sandeep's efforts

 c. Decision to travel by train and not allowing them to travel together.

 d. Sandeep's suffering from severe projectitis.

Ironically, all these decisions have been taken by operation people, whether rightly or wrongly. The irony lies in the fact that if the outcome or the fall out any such decision goes awry, the damage, often will have to be repaired by the HR functionaries as almost always those damages have HR implications which the functionaries in other areas are not equipped to handle.

vi. What lessons you learn from this case study?

The answer to this question has been distributed in the answers to all the other questions above, particularly in the previous question. Summarizing them once more will at the cost of repetition. But, at the end of the day, the gist of the lessons we learn is that management is an integrated activity and step/s taken in one functional area may have implications in other functional areas. So, in the interest of the organization as a whole, all the functionaries in different areas will have to work in unison and conjunction with one another without pointing accusing fingers at each other.

TACIT/IMPLICIT AND EXPLICIT/ ORGANIZATIONAL KNOWLEDGE

Bibekanando (that is how it is pronounced in Bengali) Mukherjee alias Billu (his nick name) was very naughty and restless in his childhood. He was sort of a dare devil and kept his mother in tenterhooks most of the time. But, surprisingly, he calmed down considerably during his adolescence and became a brilliant student by the time he became an adult. In due course, he turned out to be a solid pillar of strength for his parents to fall back upon.

Belonging to the lower middle class economic status, his parents had their own problems. His father was a diploma holder in civil engineering and could find employment intermittently in construction sites around the city on contract basis. On an average, for quite a few number of years, he was employed only for about six to seven months in a year. Life was not easy for Billu and his family of five i.e. Billu's grandmother, parents and two younger siblings, one brother and one sister. Only saving grace was the share in the ancestral property of two rooms inherited at the heart of the city.

Billu's father could put him only in a local government school with vernacular medium (Bengali), paying a nominal tuition fee. He could not afford any education more sophisticated than that. Billu, nevertheless, blossomed like a proverbial 'lotus in the pond' and became a consistent rank holder throughout and beyond i.e. up to plus two. His crowning glory was, however, a prized seat in the nearest government engineering college again with only a nominal fee. His parents were elated because putting their son in to a private engineering college was out of the question.

Billu did not let them down either. He was campus selected by a medium scale electronic industry in Ahmedabad. The company was supplying mission critical space grade electronic hardware to ISRO. In fact, Billu, from the very beginning of his engineering course hated software. Luckily, he got a hardware oriented job and for the first time in his life, stepped out of his native city for the capital city of Gujrat.

All the new recruits in engineering had to undergo a rigorous orientation cum induction training program lasting for as long as six months. As has been his wont so far, he out shown all his other batch mates by putting up a meritorious performance, picked up the intricacies of electronic system design and, up on confirmation, bagged his first professional assignment of absorbing the design and alignment of space borne trans-receivers for the 'Space Application Centre' (SAC), Ahmedabad. Six numbers of this SAC designed product will have to be supplied to SAC by his company within the coming six months. Making six numbers was no big deal but the alignment and tuning were very critical and demanded a tremendous personal professional skill.

Billu was required to be camping in SAC and trained by the SAC design engineers and after successful completion of the training had to come back to his company and deliver six sets which would undergo critical evaluation tests and quality checks as per the prescribed space standard. Billu proved himself to be fully up to the mark, absorbed the training sincerely and diligently gathered expertise, came back to his mother industry, worked hard and delivered. His sincerity and dedication were highly appreciated by both SAC and his own company bosses. As ISRO undertook more and more space missions, their dependence on trained suppliers grew higher and higher and Billu's company thought it fit to establish a separate department dedicated to space flight products and, of course, Billu was the obvious choice to head the department, albeit a bit prematurely. Quite a few eyebrows were raised, quite a few feathers were ruffled as becoming a HoD by the fourth year of service for a graduate engineer was unprecedented in the company and perhaps, that was Billu's undoing.

Before BIllu could realize and come to terms with the implications of this promotion, he was summoned by the BoD. He was profusely congratulated to start with and subsequently told to get ready to discharge managerial functions henceforth and not to limit himself to remain only a technical expert. He was destined to fulfill bigger managerial roles in the company – he was told. He was immediately required to plan for the new department in terms of its plant and machineries, other supporting infrastructure facilities, man power requirements and budgetary provisions and with revenue forecasting. He was also told, unequivocally, to identify, at his discretion, a group of engineers in house and transfer all his technical skills and expertise acquired from SAC to them so that he would be free to manage the whole department. And if such merit was not available in house, he should go for a talent hunt, find and recruit them from wherever they are. He was also expected to frequent his visit to SAC and grab more and more orders for the company using his goodwill.

Surprisingly, instead of getting encouraged, Billu was stupefied, stunned and crestfallen. He was totally unprepared for this sudden elevation and the change of his duties. He had, in fact, developed a tremendous personal attachment to the products he delivered and over the years, started believing that in a high-tech industry like his, technical skill was, by far, a supreme skill and once acquired, nobody should be forced to sacrifice it. He could not find much appeal in the functions of recruitment and getting orders and felt terribly let down. As he was submerged in his thoughts, pondering over his future, sitting in his bachelor accommodation, he could hear his native city of birth was beckoning him back. He decided to put in his papers.

Questions:

i.   What went wrong and why, instead of getting elated, Billu was depressed on his elevation. Give reasons.

There were a few reasons not far to seek. It was the ineptness of the management to have elevated Billu all on a sudden, in a hurry to create a profit center with Billu at the helm. From strategic point of view to exploit the favorable market condition without any delay, management was right. But, the management failed in taking into consideration the HR implication of its move. A product developer very often gets inescapably attached to his products and that fact should not have been ignored.

Secondly, Billu, before the elevation was at an operational level and entered middle management cadre by virtue of the promotion with the accompanying change in his duties and responsibilities. So far, he has been accustomed to high tech work all by himself. Henceforth, he would be required to get such high tech work done by others reporting to him. His performance would be judged by the performance of his sub-ordinates, a role which may not be acceptable by many at the outset.

On both these counts, he needed counseling and training. Promoting him and training him up for the new role come under the purview of HRM.

ii. Was Billu's reaction justified? Do you believe that Billu's modest upbringing was, anyway, responsible for his adverse reaction? Give reasons.

The justification for BIllu's reaction has been given in the answer to the previous question. For the second part, it can be said that, if not directly, but indirectly, Billu's upbringing could, as well, be responsible for his unfavorable reaction. Billu was brought up in an atmosphere of economic stringency. So, it can be easily guessed that he did not have cook, domestic servant maid or driver to help the family with their daily needs as is the case in many even not so affluent Indian families. Billu was accustomed to and comfortable with doing all his personal requirements himself except perhaps cooking which was presumably done by his mother. So, in short, for this elevated professional role, he needed grooming.

iii. Do you think Billu's employer was the right company for him? Give reasons.

At the very outset, it can be said that Billu was not exactly fit for a manufacturing company. A very high technology project management organization like ISRO would have been more suitable for him. In ISRO like organizations, the level of technology handled is so high that an engineer with a high qualification and long experience has to develop equipment with his own hands, may be supported by the support staff in the mundane areas. In the advanced countries where entrepreneurship flourish, there are quite a few such organizations in the private sectors whereas in a developing country like India in the private sector and hardware area such companies are very rare. There are such companies in software.

iv. Was Billu's employer right in their approach? Was it all Billu's fault?

Both these issues have been discussed in the answers to the earlier questions. Neither Billu nor his employer was exactly right. The employer was driven by pure profit motives ignoring the HR implications, a malady from which many high tech MSMEs in India suffer. On the other hand, Billu's family conditions, upbringing and value system were not conducive for is new elevated role in the managerial cadre in a high tech organization.

v. Highlight the HR issues involved in this case study. What HR lessons you derive from this case study?

This case study involves outright HR issues which have been discussed already. As far as learning lessons is concerned, we should learn that strategic managerial actions and operational measures often create situations which may have severe and at times, sinister HR implications. They have to be taken care of meticulously as and when they arise otherwise organizations would lose capable people like the protagonist Bibekanando here.

One more relevant HR issue which has not been touched upon so far is that of knowledge management. What knowledge and skill our protagonist in this case study acquired by dint of his sincerity and hard work is tacit knowledge which was confined within the acquirer. The acquirer, in the process of acquiring that knowledge, developed a sense of ownership of that expertise. But, when the employing organization wanted to capitalize on that knowledge on a larger scale and asked him to part with and disseminate that knowledge to his juniors, the protagonist resisted. The acquirer did not want to lose his supposed proprietorship of the expertise.

This is one of the major challenges in management in general and HRM in particular i.e. converting tacit knowledge acquired in the course of doing paid office work, confined within an individual to implicit knowledge which becomes the property of the organization as such and used for the overall welfare for all the stake holders of that organization without losing the original acquirer from its service.

CASE STUDY 23

BROTHERS IN ARMS/KARAN-ARJUN SYNDROME EXTENDED TO PROFESSION

Aditya Sahay and Arun Jha were close friends from the very childhood as far back in time as they themselves and even the others in the neighborhood could remember. Even their families were very close to each other. They were two Bihari brahmin families nestled in Ranchi, the capital city of today's Jharkhand. But, when these two male children were born at around the same time, the state of Jharkhand was yet to be formed. The area was a part of tribal dominated south Bihar. With the formation of Jharkhand, suddenly, the native Bihari settlers became outsiders in their own land. Anyway, that was another matter altogether.

Apart from having only one male child each, both these families had a number of other similarities. Economically, they belonged to the upper crust of the lower middle class with a strong moral value system. Aditya's father was teaching Hindi in a local primary school while Arun's father was a lower division clerk in the state government. Their work places were near their residences within cycling distance and they used to cycle daily. Their mothers were housewives, both the women used to give a lot of personal attention to their children mostly imbibing moral values and forthrightness. Their first and foremost ambition was good character and education; economic prosperity came next in order. Crash consumerism was just rearing its head those days but their families were yet to be affected.

Despite their meagre economic means, both the families dared to provide the best of education to their children. Both the boys did their schooling in a local convent school in English medium, had their moral values even more strengthened.

After completing their intermediate in science honorably, they joined the BIT in Mesra, Ranchi to do graduation in chemical engineering. Both of them also managed to get selected in the college football team and won trophies even at the interstate levels. Both of them were stars in their college and their parents had high hopes, quite reasonably. No wonder, when the recruitment company, a large scale chemical industry in the private sector from Taloja, a suburb of Mumbai (Bombay in those days) visited BIT, both of them were picked up as graduate engineer trainees. The small city boys pulled up their socks, got ready to venture into the big challenging world of Mumbai.

As they say, even if you are identical looking Siamese twins, your fates would be different. This adage came true very much for this duo. Although, they tried to maintain the trail of similarities by finding shelter in the same working boys' hostel in suburban Khar, travelling to Taloja by the company transport, their departments and bosses were different and that made their destinies also quite different. Aditya was lucky, he got posted in the product development department under a boss who was a MTech. in chemical engineering from IIT, Bombay. He had to interact with only technically qualified people and was getting along smoothly.

Arun was, however, not so lucky. He found posting in the commercial department. His job was to provide technical support to commercial transactions and his colleagues were mostly from commerce background whose conversations and parlance he neither understood nor appreciated. He felt like a fish out of water and his boss's attitude added to his misery. His boss was a commerce graduate from interior Maharashtra who used to declare openly that engineers lacked commercial sense. He also used to say that commercial transactions were the mainstream activities of a business and technical functions, could at the best, be supporting. This view was also resented by Arun very much and he used to feel humiliated.

The issue came to a flash point when, one morning, Arun's boss called him to his chamber.

Boss: "Arun, listen carefully, I am going to give you a very important assignment. Take this brief case to the airport in our company's car. Don't try to open it. Hand it over to a person who is landing from Delhi. Collect his identity and the flight details from the office."

Arun felt distinctly uncomfortable, nevertheless, got the identity of the person from the boss's PA and went down to the parking place, only to be confronted by the driver:

Driver: Oh! Sir, out of all the others, this job comes on your head! Should I tell you what is there in this briefcase? Rupees twenty-five lakhs, bribe for an industrial license. We may be intercepted and robbed by criminals on the way, but we shall be held responsible for the money. It is too risky, Sir.

Arun was stunned. He thought for a while and then went up to his boss.

Arun: I am sorry, Sir. I am an engineer. I believe I should not be used as an office boy to carry briefcases.

Boss: So, you are refusing to do this job?

Arun: I am helpless Sir. My conscience does not permit.

Boss: (red faced) Oh! That's fine. Just wait a bit and see what my conscience is asking me to do now.

Right in front of Arun, he rang up the HR manager in charge of Arun's department and upon his quick arrival at his office:

Boss: Avinash, our Arun is not happy with our company, he wants to go. Please settle his accounts immediately.

Then he turned to Arun:

Boss: Please help Avinash by submitting your papers, wish you all the best.

The matter was over within about a couple of hours. He was handed over a cheque covering three months 'advance salary for the mandatory notice period. Back to the hostel, when Aditya returned in the evening, he narrated the incident. Aditya was furious. The very next morning, he barged into the office of Arun's boss without informing his own boss as he was yet to arrive.

Aditya: Sir, I am terribly shocked by the way Arun was treated. It was unjust and I have come to express my anguish and objection.

Arun's Boss (taken aback) Anguish and objection? Oh! That's great. I see. Ram and Shyam of our company? Ram has already gone and Shyam can also follow suit, no issues. Don't worry, I shall talk to your boss.

As soon as Aditya got back to his own department, his boss called him.

Aditya's Boss: (in very bad mood) Who asked you to go and talk to Arun's boss without consulting me? This is a corporate office, not your college or home. When will you grow up? This time, I have somehow saved your job. Henceforth, be careful and behave yourself. Will you?

Aditya decided to leave the company and started applying for jobs elsewhere.

Questions:

i. Was Arun justified in his reaction? Do you believe his upbringing had anything to do with his reaction?

To do justice to this question, Arun's reaction should be divided in two parts. The first part is about his standpoint on principle and inner value system. It may, as well, be that his principles and value system did not permit him to be a privy to a mechanism for bribing and corruption. His conscience came in the way and he refused.

The second part was his approach in making his refusal effective by his articulation expressing objection. The words he used to express his objection were not appropriate and to an extent mis-leading. He brought into the picture the issue of qualification which could be misinterpreted as that engineers are too highly qualified to be as bearers of briefcases, thereby indirectly hinting that the boss was only a commerce graduate and could not comprehend the importance and gravity of an engineer.

Secondly, his reply and choice of words could also be interpreted as that he was prepared to do only those jobs connected with engineering and nothing else. The expression of this attitude made him potently unsuitable for a mid-size, albeit large scale, industry in the private sector.

Water tight and rigid compartmentalization of duties might not be feasible in private sector industries.

Thirdly, his reaction might have been prompted by mortal fear. After the driver's disclosure it was revealed that the brief case was not an ordinary one and Arun might have suffered from a terrible sense of insecurity. But, this was not understood by his boss.

On all these three counts, his non – co-operation infuriated his boss. Regarding his upbringing coming on the way, the issue has been discussed above in part one of this reply.

ii. Was the action taken by Arun's boss justified? Consider without going into the moral issues. Did he violate any management principle?

Even without going into the moral issues, it can be certainly said that the action taken by Arun's boss by removing Arun from service was not justified. He should have interpreted Arun's reaction more positively and constructively. Arun's reaction was more out of his unsuitability for the job rather than his attitude of non-co-operation. It was incumbent upon Arun's boss to identify gamut of activities for which Arun could be more suitable and could contribute to the progress of his company.

The basic principle of HR is: "Identify strength and utilize, not weakness and penalize." Even according to the four 'Ts' of HRM i.e. Transaction, Translation, Transition and Transformation, the boss as well as the HR manger failed in their duties and became unjust both to Arun and the company. They proved their professional incompetence.

iii. Was Aditya's reaction to his friend's deprivation justified? Could or should he have carried his friendship and personal relations to his office? What is your opinion?

For this question also, the answer will have two aspects, one is his inner feeling and the other is the manner in which he expressed himself and its appropriateness. His inner feeling of anguish and anger is well understood as his close childhood friend and now colleague, was treated unjustly.

But, the manner in which he gave outward expression of his anger and anguish was not appropriate in a corporate set up. In a corporate set up, professional code of conduct dictates that personal relation and friendship should be kept separate from professional relation among colleagues and the two should not be allowed to interfere with each other. In fact, in actual life this dictum is observed more by violation rather than compliance.

iv. What are the HR issues involved in this case study?

The issues pertaining to HR involved in this case study can be summarized as:

a. There is no mention about the induction training given to the new recruits before final posting. This is a must and it should cover exposing the trainees to the overall functions of the whole organization and each of its division. The respective divisional heads should address the trainees explaining the functions of his own division.

b. Sequentially, subsequent to the above, each incoming incumbent should be given a choice for the division he/she wishes to join after being fully acquainted with its function. This choice should be honored by the management as far as possible.

c. If a situation arises such that a particular division having a vacancy is not chosen by any trainee, the HR functionaries should take recourse to extensive counselling, motivating new recruits to join the division. Any misgiving/misconception in any trainee's mind regarding a particular division should be removed as far as possible.

d. The HR functionaries before plunging into recruitment, should study the man power requirements of all the divisions and chalk out 'Qualitative Requirement' in terms of qualification and experience of the incoming candidates suitable for the division concerned.

e. A candidate, once posted in a division, should be given three to six months' time to settle down. If he gets serious issues regarding compatibility with either the work content or the people, he should be transferred to other division and tried out. No newly posted incumbent should be asked to leave because of incompatibility with one divisional head.

f. There should be a grievance redressal mechanism in place maintained by the HR functionaries.

v. What are the HR lessons you derive from this case study?

This matter has been addressed, by and large, in the answer to the previous question. As a summary, we can say that this case study raises mainly three HR issues, namely: moral, incompatibility and arbitrary power. The HR functionaries should bear in mind that a new incumbent joins an organization loaded with the value system inculcated by the family during upbringing which cannot and should not be erased or obliterated overnight for the sake of the company. If there is a contrast, he should be given time to adapt. Regarding incompatibility, the issue has been addressed in the previous question.

For the third issue i.e. arbitrary power, it should be noted that a new incumbent joins the company and then subsequently is posted into a division as the whole organization is broken into divisions. No divisional head should be given arbitrary power to remove any trainee out rightly without consulting the concerned HR department which would consider various means to retain the candidate.

CASE STUDY 24

TOWERING PROBLEMS

Jagan Mohan Rao, in his mid-thirties, has been, all along, very ambitious and he dreams a lot. As an exception, he does not believe in dreaming while asleep, he can even dream while he is wide awake. Now – a – days, of course, sleep has become a rare commodity and the fond dreams have been replaced by worries. His father is a rich landowner in the coastal city of Vishakhapatnam in Andhra Pradesh. Traditionally, for generations, they are real estate owners and have been earning rental income from a number of residential and commercial properties in and around the city. Jagan has been an exception in more than one sense, he was not impressed by the idea of making a living with the rental income from the ancestral properties. He wished to live by the sweat of his brows and that became the root cause of all his present problems.

As a remarkable departure from family tradition, he went to study engineering in the neighboring town of Kakinada after his sincere attempts to join one of the five IITs those days did not succeed. Not to be left much behind, he, to some extent, made up for the loss by doing his post graduate from the nearest IIT i.e. at Kharagpur and got immediately rewarded. DLRL, Hyderabad selected him as Scientist-C from the campus. Within two years of service in DLRL, he became restless. Beaten by the entrepreneurial bug, he came back to his pavilion i.e. Vishakhapatnam. He started his own electronic industry. His father also helped him by standing guarantee for the big loan he took from the State Bank of Hyderabad. His father's huge real estate and his own qualification helped him a lot in avoiding mortgaging properties to the bank and getting the loan at a concessional rate of interest.

He was also lucky by enlisting the services of his wife Savitha, MBA in Finance and HR from XIMB, Bhubaneshwar, the capital city of Orissa, within a few hours from their town by train. Jagan, from the contemplating stage itself, wanted a labour intensive industry rather than a capital intensive manufacturing industry in high tech electronics. The industry of the husband-wife team "Galaxy Communication" was engaged in erection, commissioning and installation of communication towers i.e. repeater stations for the cellular service providers for the city and neighbourhood. Soon, galaxy grew in leaps and bounds, rather a bit too prematurely and swelled to 713 people on rolls. Jagan wanted a labour intensive but high – tech industry and got it. But, along with his industry and its size, his nightmare also multiplied.

Their workforce mostly comprised of wireless/radio technicians recruited from the local ITIs and a few graduate engineers. They were mostly on out-bound duties, directly commuting to the customers' premises from their residences and reporting there, on site. In fact, there was not much interaction between the management and the work force. Management took direct feedback from the customers themselves which used to be mostly negative. Jagan thought that the feedbacks directly from the customers would be more authentic. Actual difficulties faced by the workforce were mostly unknown to Jagan. He was also in the dark regarding how the customers behaved with his work force and vice-versa. Presumably, on account of not being able to deliver, while their issues were not being addressed by the management, the employees were resigning in large numbers, attrition rate was very high.

Savitha, looking after both finance and HR felt overloaded with the ever-growing demands of working capital management and was out of depth in HR ; the function was entrusted to a middle-aged professional who was a commerce graduate with a diploma in HR. This manager could, at his best, evolve certain metrics for performance evaluation and left every decision having financial implication to the Director, Finance i.e. Savitha. After an extensive brainstorming, the two directors were told by the HR team that either the employees be trained in the domain the customers want them to work or several projects will have to be withdrawn. The director duo also found that the morale of the employees was low on account of a multitude of reasons. The HR team, through an internal survey had assessed the same and reported to the directors. They also suggested a multitude of changes to ensure control on attrition together with higher morale for employees.

Questions:

i. Can you sense any inadequacy in the functioning of HR in the company? Yes, the HR functions in the company was not properly looked after. In fact, most of the business entities in the MSME sector in India suffer from a woefully inadequate attention to the HR area. The attention and emphasis of the management in this sector get mostly concentrated in marketing and finance areas and HR gets neglected and overlooked. In a country like India where unemployment is rampant, such attitude of the management is but natural.

But, that is nothing short of a blunder. By astute marketing, we can get customers and their orders. To deliver/service those orders, we need quality and motivated manpower. In the absence of that, customers won't get what they want in time and the company's revenue earning will get adversely affected jeopardizing cash inflow and finance. So, there is no escape from the fact that with an inadequate attention to HR, a company can't survive.

To be more specific in this case, the inadequacies in HR can be summarized as:

a. With the rapid expansion of cellular networks in India, the market conditions were very favourable for the service providers. The company grew manifolds in a very short period and the field strength grew beyond seven hundred. The company's HR functions was not bolstered adequately to take care of such a huge manpower and the personnel felt neglected and uncared for.

b. HR was looked after by one of the founding directors on a part time basis. Her main attention was on finance. The company should have inducted another director/senior functionary to look after HR independently.

c. When the field staff were reporting directly to the customers to save commuting time and expenses, the company depended on one – sided feedback from the customers. The company should have recruited and deputed qualified supervisory staff in field to oversee the work and report regularly to the company on a day to day basis. The field staff also could have discussed their grievances/difficulties on the spot with the supervisors and get immediate redressal.

ii. Identify the strengths of the company. Why HR was weak amidst those strengths?

The main strengths of the company were its founding directors who were professionally qualified and dedicated. They were professionals first and businessmen next. They were also from an affluent back ground with a solid financial support from family. This combination of the favourable factors is quite rare.

Their weakness lay in the fact that technically qualified people very often fail to understand the importance and intricacies of HR. They tend to believe, albeit falsely, that the personnel they hire will be as dedicated and engaged as they are to the company. Engaging a workforce and keeping them motivated to achieve the company's goals is really a challenge.

iii. If you were the HR head, what type of training and development plan and strategy you would suggest to the two directors?

As it appears from the narration of the case, the employees were mostly from technical back ground. The company was also technology based, so the training for the new recruits should be a two-tier arrangement i.e. technical as well as behavioral.

The manpower hired was mostly from the ITIs and hence they would be very young and immature. To start with, there should be induction training in which they should be introduced to the company they have joined in terms of its line of business and the career and growth prospects and also its HR policies. This induction training can be given by the directors themselves.

Secondly, they should be trained in the specific area of technology involved and its intricacies and challenges. They should also be exposed to the specifications and critical technical parameters of the system they would be installing. This element of training can be imparted by experts hired from outside on contract basis.

The third element, no less crucial, would be exposure to the customer profile and how to behave with them so that they are satisfied and not antagonized. This training should also be imparted by professional behavioral trainers

iv. Do the employees need certain behavioral training to improve their morale?

As has been covered in the answer to the previous question, the new recruits do require behavioral training. That is not exactly aimed at improving their morale but to acquire the skill of dealing with the customer effectively. The employees are getting demoralized because their difficulties are not addressed and their grievances are not redressed. The remedy, as has been suggested earlier, lies in appointing supervisors as intermediaries between the management and the workers who would act as the spokespersons on behalf of the workers.

The fact of the matter is that customer is the king and their behavior can't be controlled by the management. Some of the customers may be very rude and arrogant. Nevertheless, they also will have to be pacified and satisfied at the interest of the company, otherwise they may poison the other customers' minds.

Gaining customer satisfaction, is a subtle art; the field staff have to learn it.

v. What lessons in HR you derive from this case study?

For a practitioner and student of HR, there are a few lessons to learn in this case study:

a. The field staff should not be left at the mercy, whims and fancy of the customer. There should be management representative present at the work spot.

b. The productivity and efficiency of the workers should be monitored at the work spot after laying down suitable standard. Higher productivity should be rewarded and lower one punished.

c. Suitable incentive and bonus scheme for the field workers will have to be worked out.

CASE STUDY 25

JOINT VENTURE BLUES IN GOVERNMENT SECTOR – A FEW LESSONS TO LEARN

Intriguing are the ways in which the technology based organizations under the government work. Sometimes, it appears that they relish swimming in the ocean of egocentricity with scanty regard for the outcome i.e. the result. Take for example, the case of a renowned R & D organization engaged in developing rockets and missiles for military and space application which is exclusively reserved for the national government to venture into. Private enterprises are statutorily excluded.

The organization under our study here was renowned for its brilliance in R & D but had inadequate manufacturing expertise and infrastructure. When our defense expenditure shot up to pierce the roof (courtesy our friendly neighboring countries), there were intense R & D activities which required robust and matching manufacturing support for the prototype and zero series production. Ministry of defense was frantically looking for a company which could match up to the requirements and identified Asian Electronics, a central public sector unit, as the right partner. Of course, the search was limited within the government companies only because the policies were not liberalized yet to involve the private sector, those days.

The arrangement was to be a joint venture between a government concern/ organization under the ministry of defense and a government company also under the same ministry i.e. ministry of defense production to be more precise. It was decided to open a dedicated division in the manufacturing company to cater to the requirements and hence, the division had to be headed by a senior official from Asian Electronics i.e. the host company. There was one more valid reason. The entire capital investment to set up the division was incurred by the manufacturing company i.e. Asian Electronics, so they had the legitimate right to have full control over the division. However, the R & D partner was not that comfortable with the arrangement. They wanted someone of their own to head the division.

In fact, the arrangement i.e. the joint venture, however merited by the exigencies of circumstances, was flawed, ab – initio, mainly due to the mismatch of attitude, culture and value system prevalent mostly in government organizations. The highlights of the attitude of the R & D organization could be summarized as:

i. In making an equipment/device, design is the main thing. Making that is a subsidiary issue, any mediocre mind can do that.

ii. Manufacturing is a mundane activity, bereft of any creativity like designing.

iii. Mediocre minds should be allowed to interact only with their ilk i.e. another such mediocre mind.

iv. Manufacturer is the gainer economically in this game of joint venture. Their profitability and turnover is increasing.

On the other hand, Asian Electronics had a view like:

i. A design is an intellectual paper work. Any design to be worth its name, should pass the litmus test of producibility, if the product has to see the light of the day ultimately.

ii. Any design may have to be redesigned to ensure/augment its producibility.

iii. During this redesign phase, constant interaction with the original designer may be needed.

iv. In this joint venture, both the parties are benefitted. The designer will get the product when needed and the manufacturer will gain revenue, it is a win-win game.

The real ruckus commenced when the designer had to depute their personnel in the joint venture at the manufacturer's division. All the so called brilliant minds of the designer were pre-occupied and none could be spared, only the mediocre minds could be deputed for liaising which was crucial as direct access of the manufacturer to the design engineers was denied. But, interpreting high technology designs by absorbing the idea and transferring the same to the manufacture also demanded a good lot of commitment and competence. Mediocre minds were found lacking in these qualities. But, the matter came to a head on administrative issues:

i. Government employees are accustomed to report to seniors only when the senior' salary was higher than theirs.

ii. Central government employees work only five days in week, central government companies work all the six days.

iii. Central government employees work from 9 AM to 5 PM and for R & D, government industries work from 8 AM to 4 PM shift.

The net resultant effect was that, personnel deputed to the manufacturing company were attending duties from 9 AM to 4 PM and not coming on Saturdays. Liaising work suffered every day and every week. The last straw on the proverbial camel's back was the announcement of revised salary for the central government employees as per the recommendation of a pay commission. The salaries of all the central government officers deputed to the manufacturer's concern became higher than that of the head of the division itself, all of them refused to report to him.

The manufacturer, even after making a huge capital investment, decided to close down the division.

Questions:

i. Was the joint venture ill-conceived by the authorities? Was it not realistic?

The idea of this joint venture made a lot of sense and was not at all ill – conceived. The joint venture was based on the principle of positive synergy i.e. combining strengths of R & D and manufacturing that complement each other. A research organization and a manufacturing industry under the government of India and under the same ministry, need not and should not work in isolation and re-invent the wheel, at the cost of the exchequer, of course. They can always come together on a particular project basis and thereby save a lot of time and money and resources for the country.

It was nothing unrealistic. As the field in which these two entities were functioning happen to be the exclusive preserve of the government of India and private plyers were barred as a matter of policy, the arrangement seemed, at the outset, quite realistic.

ii. What is exactly the difference between a government concern/organization and a government company?

Here what is meant by a government concern or organization is a government department, directly under the government of India, coming under a particular ministry, depending on its activity like the railways and defense. These departments are headed by an IAS or allied services officer i.e. a government executive. On the other hand, a government company is a legal entity registered under the Company Law whose liabilities are limited by shares as per the relevant provisions of the company law. When more than fifty percent, by value, of these shares are held by government, the company becomes a government company. They are also known as public sector companies. When government decides to liquidate its holding on a government company by releasing these shares to the common men to buy in the Indian capital market, the exercise is called 'privatization.'

Both these two entities i.e. a government department and a government company have a lot of similarities and differences. The similarity is that, in both these entities, employees' jobs are secured. Also, very often than otherwise, their work cultures are also similar. The difference lies in the salary and perquisite structure for the employees. Direct government employees are traditionally paid significantly more than their public sector counterpart for the same level of responsibility.

iii. What could be responsible for the attitude of both the parties involved? Their approach to the issue of this joint venture is the outcome of their attitude and outlook. Their attitude and outlook are, in turn, the results of their work culture and value systems. To highlight the contrast, it can be cited that the defense R & D organization was mainly a project management organization whereas the manufacturing company was a production management organization. The emphasis in the R & D organization was timely completion of the project at any cost. The production organization had to be both time and cost conscious. Time was money for them and attendance time discipline was very important. That was not the value system for the R & D organization where flexible timing of attendance is sometimes resorted to.

The R & D organization was a cost center for the government whereas the production organization was a profit center albeit with a social service motive.

The main culprit as an impediment to their joint progress was the attitude of superiority on the part of the R & D organization coupled with their opportunistic stance with regard to different timings and higher salary. Mainly, the basic spirit of working together was absent.

iv. What could be a viable solution to this issue?

The viable solution was not far to seek. As both of them were under the same ministry, the ministry of defense should have put its foot down. The concerned secretaries at the south block could call the heads of both these organizations and given them a thorough dressing down emphasizing that they were required to iron out their differences and work together and deliver in the greater interest of the country as a whole. It was a question of the country's defense and tax payers' money.

v. Was the conflict a HR issue?

Yes, indeed. The conflict manifested itself into differences in work culture, time discipline, seniority and reporting pattern, all of which pertain to HR and OB.

vi. What can be the lessons in HR & OB we can derive from this case study?

a. The higher ups with the HR managers of both the organizations should have conducted a joint counselling session for the officials regarding the importance and the working arrangements for the venture.

b. The timing of the host organization should have been made binding all in the new division.

c. Seniority and gravity of a rank should have been determined by responsibility and not salary.

d. The divisional head was to be regarded as the boss irrespective of the lopsided salary structure

CASE STUDY 26

GLIMPSES OF STRATEGIC HUMAN RESOURCES MANAGEMENT

Hindusthan Electronics Ltd. (HEL), established in 1954, has been one of the largest conglomerate in professional electronics in the whole of Asia. Although in the public sector, headquartered in Bangalore under the ministry of defense, it has never been in the red since inception, courtesy our friendly neighbouring countries. Whenever there has been any conflict across our border, HEL's balance sheet has shown remarkable improvements. It has been faithfully fulfilling its purpose of formation. Starting from an equipment assembler for the Radio Corporation of America (RCA) in India, now it makes even giant Radars for both its military and civilian customers i.e. the country's armed forces, civil aviation and the meteorological departments. This diversification and capacity expansion has taken about four decades of dedication to quality, technology and innovation.

But, of course, this glorious journey towards professional excellence has taken place not without its due quota/share of hiccups. Ironically, HEL for a long time since beginning has been keeping a lot of faith in the managerial caliber of bureaucrats both with and without uniforms. The Board of Directors has been dominated by retired and about to retire bureaucrats or military officers. It used to be a safe haven for very senior central government or even state government officials or military officers from all the three wings i.e. Army, Navy and Air Force who could not be promoted further in their respective careers.

This end of the journey solace or succour to the retiring officials whose further upward march in their respective mainstream career was highly improbable, had a few ramifications like:

i. As the lion's share of the orders was coming from the armed forces and the civil aviation, any senior officer retiring from these service areas would be in a better position to liaise if he was at the helm of affairs here.

ii. As these senior people were brought up in the armed forces, they could bring about order and enforce a sense of discipline among the work force.

iii. As these officers were at the fag – end of their career, having only about two to five years of career left at the maximum, most of them were in the mood of winding up and lacked initiative and vision.

iv. As they were rank outsiders as far as the company was concerned, there was serious cultural mismatch with the rest of the officers down the line and, as such, they had to function confined in their isolated ivory towers.

v. As these officers at the senior most positions were thrust upon the company, the other officers, mostly highly technically qualified who have been with the company for more than three decades, found their upward movement blocked beyond General Manager level and this policy became a serious demotivating factor.

The proverbial last straw on the camel's back was when an officer from the Indian Audit and Account Services was appointed as the Director, Finance at the tender age of forty-five, when a host of officers from technical cadre, a few of them even from the IITs, were struggling to get directorship even at the age of fifty-five. Most of these officers decided to leave, but were waiting for the right opportunity to come by; and it came sooner than expected in the form of a policy of 'Voluntary Retirement Scheme'(VRS) introduced by the company. The level just below the BoD i.e. General Manager was almost deserted and the company was staring at a managerial vacuum.

There was one more sinister fall out of the policy of appointing senior bureaucrats and military officers at the helm. The company's product diversification was seriously jeopardized. These officers at the top were familiar with and interested only in the line of products they had been using in their mainstream career and did not venture into any new product areas due to lack of ideas, familiarity and risk perception. But, when the company, upon clearance from the concerned ministry, relented to change the HR policy and appointed an insider who rose from the rank and file, as the CEO, there was a sea change. This new incumbent immediately went into manufacturing components and VLSI by going into a technical collaboration plus a sizeable buy-back with M/s Fairchild, an American MNC, a giant in the field This strategic and smart move by the CEO, however, opened on its wake, a flood gate of controversies:

i. As there was a gigantic cash outflow to procure the plant and machinery and infrastructure, amortization was a big problem and the company's hitherto comfortable and tranquil balance sheet got hit badly for several years to come. The company, for the first time, missed its 20% bonus payment to the employees which it had been doing since inception.

ii. There was a huge HRM challenge, as making components and VLSI was a different ball game altogether; the existing in – house expertise was unsuitable. Fresh manpower was required and no suitable expert was ready to join given the existing salary structure.

iii. A few engineers had to be sent abroad to the collaborator in USA for advanced training.

iv. Salaries had to revised upwards. Both these moves further damaged the balance sheet.

v. The recognized trade unions, as many as three of them, served strike notice as all the profits made by the company's equipment division could not compensate for the loss suffered due to the new component division. The workers of the equipment division were aggrieved,

vi. The company contemplated declaring lock out to counter the impending strike.

vii. The American MNC, the collaborator, threatened to withdraw the buy-back support if there was a lock out as contemplated.

The management was left wondering if they had done the right thing by appointing an insider as the CEO.

Questions:

i.   Do you support government of India's policy of appointing CEOs for a manufacturing company out of its retiring military or civilian officers? A blunt, straight forward and categorical answer to this question may not be appropriate here. The practice of appointing retired or retiring government officers as CEOs of central government's manufacturing industries has got its merits and demerits. If we look at this issue from purely the "principles of HRM" point of view, this practice has more demerits than merits. As has been mentioned in the narration of this case, the principal merits of appointing bureaucrats with or without uniforms, in the manufacturing industries are experience, discipline and better liaising with the government. On the other hand, the demerits are cultural mismatch, rigidity and lack of innovativeness. The most dangerous demerit is yet to be mentioned i.e. the feeling among the rank and file that however meritorious you are, the topmost position is not for you, it is for an outsider. That is the principal drawback of this HR policy.

ii. Was there any other way the government could utilize the experience and services of its senior officers for enriching its manufacturing activities without substantially demoralizing the insiders? Of course, there are a few indirect ways in which the government could have a cake and eat it too:

a.   For better liaising, each major customer segment i.e. army, navy, air-force, para military, civil aviation and Met department can have their respective liaising cells set up in the supplier industry to look after their interests and constantly interact with the line managers of the host industry. These cells should be staffed by senior officers from the respective customer organizations deputed at those cells. These officers so deputed would have advisory and not executive powers over the officers of the host industry.

b.   Very senior officers from the customer organizations mentioned above should also be deputed as Directors in the Board of Directors so that appropriate policies safeguarding and serving their interests could be formulated and adopted. As this is a current practice, it should be continued.

   c. To enforce, ensure and promote a sense of discipline, the top levels of the middle management cadre can as well be manned by officers deputed from the armed forces. Voluntarily retired officers from the armed forces can be absorbed at this level for permanent appointment provided they are at the right age. Care should be taken to see that these appointments should not jeopardize the promotion prospects of insiders who have grown with the company.

iii. Was the government officer turned CEO justified in sticking to the line of business in equipment manufacturing as they did? Was it a limitation or a considered judgement?

The conservative approach by the military officer turned CEO in sticking to the familiar line of equipment manufacture might be out of his limitation, but, eventually proved right for the organization at this juncture. The fall out of the drastic and daring move by the insider CEO is there for everyone to see. This strategic diversification has virtually opened a proverbial Pandora's box.

iv. Was the new incumbent CEO justified in diversifying into components and VLSI? Was it a strategic blunder?

Technically, he might be right, but not managerially. Before diversifying into a product line for which the technology and capital equipment requirements were totally different, he should have undertaken a strategic restructuring of the company.

v. How the complicated situation arising in the wake of the diversification could be mitigated/salvaged?

As has been indicated in the answer to the previous question, the situation could be and still can be salvaged by a strategic re-structuring of the company. The company should restructure itself into a holding company/subsidiary company pattern. The two divergent divisions i.e. equipment division and the component division will be two different subsidiary companies under the same umbrella holding company. The Board of Directors of the subsidiary companies will be determined and constituted by the BoD of the holding company. The profit and loss accounts and the balance sheets of the subsidiary companies will be made differently and independent of each other so that the profit made by the equipment division need not be appropriated against the loss made by the component division. The heavy capital outlay made for the component factory will be made independently and will not affect the balance sheet of the equipment factory.

Most importantly, the equipment factory will show profit as it has been making consistently and bonus can be given to its workers as usual. As the component factory is a new factory, it need not pay bonus until it breaks even and makes profit.

vi. What lessons in strategic management you derive from this case study? A keen student of management can learn useful lessons from this case study:

a. If the customer community mix is dominated by a few powerful organizations placing the lion's share of the orders, it makes sense to involve them in management.

b. This involvement of the representatives of the customer organization in management, however, has to be done very cautiously and imaginatively so as not to hurt the sentiments and sensibilities, also not to jeopardize the future prospects of the existing insider line managers.

c. To avoid the ominous prospects of culture clash, these representative officers of the customer organization/s should not be appointed as line managers. They should be accommodated only in staff positions. The organization structure should be designed meticulously so that suitable staff positions are created from where these officers brought in from outside, can discharge their respective functions effectively. This managerial maneuver calls for a good lot of astuteness and dexterity on the part of the management.

d. As far as the diversification into component manufacturing brought about by the new incumbent is concerned, it can be termed as 'backwards horizontal integration' in strategic management parlance. Normally, for such types of corporate maneuvers, opening a new division to accommodate the new activity should be sufficient. But, here, in this case, the challenge was more acute because of the wide differences in technology, capital equipment, trained manpower, financing patterns, profitability, bonus payments etc.it is advisable to go for separate subsidiaries to facilitate independent functioning as far as possible.

vii. Other than strategy, does this case study imply any lesson in HRM for you?

Yes, indeed. To be accurate, it can be said that most of the lessons this case study offers are in the realm of strategic HRM. Apart from that, this case study also teaches us the fact that management, after all, is an integrated concept. The issue to start with, was concerned with facilitating marketing functions which called for accommodating outsiders in key positions. This move had its own HR implications.

This HR implications can be split into two distinct phases: Before diversification and after diversification. The issues in both these phases have been adequately covered in the answers to the questions above and need not be repeated here.

CASE STUDY 27

ENTREPRENEURSHIP ZEAL AND A GARLAND OF THORNS

Aloke Shukla's enthusiasm and zest were quite contagious and that was one aspect on which his detractors and compatriots were unanimous. A positive thinker of the first order, it was virtually impossible to discourage him about anything. Even such a vivacious zealot felt crestfallen, such was the power of circumstances. Aloke Shukla, hailing from a capital city located almost at the center of India, i.e. Bhopal, he had been working in one of the R & D departments of Gemini Electronics for the last about fifteen years. After completing several important projects successfully, he built up a glorious track record for himself and had a bright future of occupying key position had he continued. But, he did not.

Though apparently and outwardly, he was totally dedicated to his official duties, within himself, he was yearning to become an entrepreneur. He always wanted to be his own boss. However, he believed that one had to gain a good deal of corporate experience and also accumulate resources i.e. saving, before turning an entrepreneur. He was patiently waiting for a breakthrough. Providence provided him opportunity albeit from an altogether unexpected quarter at last. India turned nuclear at that time and as a retaliation, USA put an embargo on export of their critical electronic hardware products to be used in India's defense equipments. Gemini Electronics was staring at a situation of stoppage of production on account of non-availability of imported parts and components. Hunt for an alternative supplier from all over the world was on, but not with much success.

As a parallel measure, Gemini Electronics was exploring the feasibility of developing indigenous capability of making these vital components economically within India. As the components were high technology based, economics dictated that the industry should have been in the MSME sector run by qualified engineer/s. Gemini Electronics gave a clarion call to all its engineers at the middle level who could turn an entrepreneur and take up the challenge. Aloke took it as a god-sent opportunity to fulfil his long cherished ambition and responded to the call. A formal resignation from the existing employment was needed as a prerequisite for empanelment as a registered supplier. Aloke promptly complied with. But then came up the other thorny issues.

Gemini Electronics had a particular practice for issuing capital test equipments to its engineers. All the constituent R & D departments of the company were engaged in design and development of the state of the art communication equipments for professional customers. These R & D activities were heavily dependent on use of costly state of the art capital equipments, test instruments etc. imported from advanced countries like USA, UK, France, Germany, Italy and japan. These capital equipments used to be procured by the 'capital equipments purchase committee' constituted by the management every year. This committee used to ask for purchase requests from the various user R & D departments and these requests were required to be endorsed by the respective divisional heads. Once an equipment lands up in a division, it would be issued to only one engineer against his signature who would be held responsible for its maintenance and upkeep. Though the equipment would be required to be used by many engineers working in the same department, safety, security and traceability of the equipment would be the responsibility of only the engineer who got it issued in his name. That was the prevailing practice in the company.

Our Aloke Shukla, due to his enthusiasm and zeal, always took initiative in getting such capital equipment issued in his name without much discrimination and caution. There were several such equipments running into crores of Rupees in value, he drew during his career spanning fifteen years. Now that he had resigned, he had to return all those equipments to get relieved from the company. By frantic last minute effort, he could trace only four of them while the balance three remained untraced. During this trying period, he also observed a very strange phenomenon. All his colleagues of so many years were suddenly cold, aloof and withdrawn in their behavior with him. Some of them even stopped talking to him. He had to struggle all alone in tracing the equipments. Even his own boss also refused to help him.

His employer asked him to make down payments of the depreciated book value of these three equipments as a necessary pre-condition for getting relieved. The amount ran into several lakhs of Rupees, sufficient to make a big dent in his entire life savings which definitely he could not afford. Our enthusiastic, zealous and zestful Aloke Shukla was then staring at an uncertain future.

Questions:

    i.   Was the company right in its approach in encouraging its own engineers to come out and start their own industry? What could be the merits and demerits of this initiative?

This is by all means, a bold and unusual move by the management. This kind of management initiative would definitely be riddled with controversies. Whether the company was right or wrong can be elucidated by enumerating is merits and demerits:

Merits:

    a.   As tomorrow's supplier is today's insider, he is familiar with the quality norms and the culture of his future customer and the present employer. So, liaising would be better.

    b.   The supplier does not have to hunt for orders as they are more or less assured provided he does not take the customer for granted and maintains sound professional relations.

    c.   As he is an employee of the organization today, he has some loyalty towards his employer. Tomorrow, when he becomes a supplier, despite the fact that then he will be an independent businessman, he may still maintain to some extent his past loyalty and it may be expected that he may be at the organization's beck and call so that he rises to the occasion in case of emergencies, crises or urgent needs.

    d.   As his superiors and bosses of today are going to place orders to him tomorrow, he may be called for any discussion and negotiation at the convenience of the purchaser rather than the supplier. Had he been an unconnected supplier, he may not oblige.

e. His today's employer and tomorrow's customer may expect some preferential treatment over any other customers.

So, it appears that the merits are obvious and material, but the demerits would be subtle and mostly psychological:

a. To a third party, it may appear that this particular insider/supplier is unduly favoured over other suppliers by virtue of his past connections and the whole arrangement will betray bias. The other suppliers, if any, would get demoralized.

b. Today's insider/supplier's erstwhile colleagues who are continuing to be in service of the company, would also get demoralized by the attention and prominence this supplier gets as 'á man of the moment.' They may start feeling that they could have also done the same thing to gain importance, otherwise, they are overlooked and neglected.

c. The company's external auditors may raise objections when they discover that this particular supplier is grabbing all the orders ignoring the others. They may smell connivance and may insist on getting three valid quotations from three distinctly different suppliers and negotiated minimum price.

To summarize, it can be said that these demerits are not exactly applicable here as the parts purchased are imported and the supplying country has refused to supply and there is no other contending supplier. So, it can be concluded that, notwithstanding the insiders' sentiments, the management was right.

ii. Was Aloke Shukla with all his enthusiasm and zeal, right in his approach in responding to the call positively? Should he have been more cautious and discreet in his approach?

Given to understand that the situation needed desperate, bold and spirited measures and also that Aloke Shukla was yearning to turn an entrepreneur, what he did, by all means, was justified. So, he did not display any indiscretion or lack of caution in responding to the call of the management which was the right thing for him to do.

But, his indiscretion and lack of caution lay in the fact that he was not aware of the rules and regulations of his employer binding him on the issue of capital equipments he was drawing in his name for the use of the whole department. The issue came to a head when he resigned and was leaving the employment prematurely. Had he not resigned and continued in his service up to his retirement, the same issue would have come up then. Of course, the amount involved then would have been nominal because of erosion of book value due to depreciation.

iii. Was the company right in its practice of issuing capital equipments the way it did? Could it be done in a more sensible way?

Yes, as per the concepts of management, it could be done in a more sensible way. All the constituent departments in the organization would have to be allotted cost center numbers by the cost accounting department for booking and ascertaining the cost, department wise. The capital equipments needed for the functioning of the department should be issued against this particular cost center number and not against any individual engineer working in the department. The overall responsibility of allotting these equipments belonging to the department to various engineers for their respective official work should be with the department head. The responsibility of availability, upkeep and maintenance and movement of these equipments should also lie with the department head.

When a particular head of any such department gets changed due to transfer, retirement or resignation, the new incumbent in his place will have to take over the responsibility.

iv. What could be the reasons for the strange behavior of Aloke's colleagues once he resigned?

As per the concepts of management science, such behavior on the part of the colleagues of Aloke was not strange at all. It appeared strange to Aloke because he confused between true friends and colleagues. A colleague is not a friend, he is an associate and the association are due to the employment i.e. working together. A true friend never deserts us irrespective of any adverse condition whereas a colleague who is an associate will no longer remain friendly when such association is snapped or broken. When Aloke opted for entrepreneurship and resigned his job, he no longer remained as a colleague and hence his erstwhile associates also turned their faces.

There was yet another curious reason why they behaved the way they behaved. They no longer wished to be identified as an associate of Aloke in the eyes of the management. Their behavior was aimed at conveying to the management the message that though Aloke's loyalty to the organization became divided after his resignation, their loyalty was intact and they deserved further promotion and growth in their career.

v. What are the lessons in HRM you derive from this case study?

There are a number of good lessons we can learn from this case study:

a. First and foremost, the company should overhaul its rules and regulations regarding issuing capital equipments to the different departments for official use. Issuing a costly capital goods meant for use for the whole department to individual engineers was improper and leads to unnecessary victimization as was evidenced in this case. Though such decision does not pertain to the realm of HR alone, it has a tremendous HR implication.

b. The company, henceforth, should not wait for a crisis situation to develop before making a clarion call to its engineers to turn entrepreneur. It should be taken as a policy by the HR functionaries to identify engineers who are entrepreneurial attitudinally and offer them opportunities with orders to open their respective industrial units.

c. The company should be sensitive to the sensibilities and apprehensions of those engineers who do not respond to their clarion call to turn entrepreneur as it is not everybody's cup of tea. They should be given the confidence that their career interests would be adequately looked after by the management.

d. A high tech company which depends heavily on imported parts should take extraordinary initiative in indigenization to overcome their dependence on foreign countries whose export policies may shift due to political exigencies.

CASE STUDY 28

HAPPY MARRIAGE AND SUBSEQUENT CAREER BLUES

At long last, Sangameshwar heaved a sigh of relief, he was getting married, so his father has written to him. Those were the days before this cell-phone and internet era and one had to depend only on letters. Sangameshwar never knew a letter could be so sweet. The eldest of six children of his father living in Raipur of today's Chhattisgarh, Sangameshwar, an engineering graduate from BIT, Mesra, Ranchi, felt like a fish out of water when he landed in Bangalore being campus selected by M/s. Gemini Electronics. The job was really good for a bright poor boy from a lower middle-class family like his.

He was finding it really tough to cope up with the unfamiliar and alien culture, language and food habits in a city in South India. During his school days at home, he was never allowed to visit the kitchen zealously guarded by his mother and sisters. He used to be only the passive beneficiary of its outcome. But, now he had to cook his own meal for dinner which he has been doing for the last about a decade without a break since he landed in Bangalore. His father retired from the state government service with a meagre salary within just one year of Sangameshwar getting employed. The economic burden of the whole family, of two younger brothers and three sisters, all studying, fell on his tender shoulders.

He stood, rock steady, by his father in those difficult days, till his two younger brothers finished college and got employed and the eldest sister finished college and got married. The burden came down substantially and then one beautiful afternoon the letter came informing him that a girl had been seen for him by his parents and he had to rush home to give his assent. For a change, the postman carrying the letter seemed like an angel without wings to him.

However, notwithstanding the rosy things that were about to happen in his personal life, his professional life was getting more and more demanding by the day. He happened to be the only senior engineer in his group who was yet to get married. The other seniors had their own families to look after. He used to be asked to go on tough field trials all over India whenever such need arose. He also never used to mind because going for trial outstation meant relief from having to cook your own dinner-he used to convince himself. But those carefree liberal days would have to change now – he thought.

His father wrote to him further that Sangameshwar would not need to visit his home town twice for marriage i.e. one for seeing the girl and the next for marriage. He could come only once and if he agreed, father would arrange for the marriage within just three days, so that he could return to work once for all with his wife. Sangam liked the idea and applied for leave of about fifteen days covering marriage and a short honeymoon trip to some exotic locale. His boss sanctioned the leave. But, just then there was a bolt from the blue. One of the equipments, deployed in the border area had failed and someone had to go and set it right. Sangam was an expert in attending to such emergencies.

His boss told him: "Draw advance TA/DA for about a month, rush to the spot, attend to the fault and then go home to get married straight. You need not report to the HQ and then again go on leave. Finish both of them together in one go. Of course, this is only a suggestion for you to save time. The final decision is yours."

"Not a bad idea" – Sangam thought and did exactly as told. A movement order was prepared empowering him to draw Travelling and Daily Allowances for about a month and he rushed to Jodhpur where the faulty equipment was brought from Rajasthan border. He attended to the work, heart and soul, within about ten days he completed the work, flew home, got married, went to honeymoon and came back to Bangalore all smile. Bangalore had two things waiting for him – a grand party from his colleagues and a warning notice from the administration.

The charge was that he drew advance amount more than double what was exactly required and kept the balance with him unauthorizedly for such a long time.

As per the prevailing rules, he was required to close/settle the pending TA/DA advance account within fifteen days of completing the outstation official work which, however, he was not aware of, neither his boss had told him while planning his leave program. This lapse and the consequent penalty constituted a negative mark on his career records which might come on the way to his promotion to the managerial cadre provided he would be otherwise eligible for it in future. That was the first time our Sangam thought of leaving the company, which eventually he did availing himself of the very first opportunity he got and his employer lost a dedicated, sincere and capable engineer with so many years of productive contribution.

Questions:

i. Was Sangameshwar himself responsible for his own predicament? How?
Yes, to some extent, Sangam himself displayed a degree of carelessness. He was expert of equipment trials and was accustomed to going for it often to various fields. He should have made himself familiar with all the prevailing rules and regulations regarding advance drawing of traveling and daily allowances and the penal provisions for its breach.

In anybody's service career for that matter, capability, integrity, sincerity and dedication are not just enough. An astute and smart functionary should be cautious and informed enough to protect his interest and safeguard his career prospects from penalty for any breach or violation however unintentional it might be.

But, ironically, he was not alone to share the blame for what had happened to him, there were others.

ii. Was the management at fault in any way? The company has lost a sincere and capable executive.
Yes, of course. The job of the management does not stop at making rules/regulations to safeguard its interest, wait for its violation and then dole out penalties and thereby destroy career and morale. It has, by all

means, to be more constructively proactive in administering rules and regulations it promulgates.

The first and foremost duty of a prudent management would be, to be proactive enough to identify those officers who are more prone to violate the provisions of the relevant rules and regulations because of the frequency and nature of their official work and make them aware of the consequences of a possible breach under the exigencies of circumstances.

At the end of the day, let us not forget that identifying violations and administering penalty is not the only job of HRM, it has to have a commitment towards the operational progress of the whole organization for the sake of virtually everybody.

iii. Was the suggestion given by Sangam's boss, right? Could he be faulted? As per the provisions of the TA/DA rules of the company, his suggestion could be faulted. He made the suggestion to Sangam in the right spirit to help him save time and money. He, himself, does not seem to have been aware of the rules and offered a suggestion which had violation inherent in it. But, at the end, he could not be framed as his suggestion had a safety rider i.e. Sangam had to make choice and be held responsible for it.

iv. What HR lessons you learn from this case study?

There are quite a few object lessons we can learn from this case study:

a. Firstly, a mid – sized company like Gemini Electronics should identify its key personnel who would be the future leaders and groom them by extensive counselling. Future leaders are to be created by meticulous pre-planning; they may not sprout out of no-where by chance as and when the need arises. This grooming by counselling has to be done surreptitiously and the sessions contents are to be designed by the HR department but administered by the operation bosses. These sessions should contain extensive coverage and exposure to the pertinent rules and regulations and penal provisions. This grooming should not draw public attention.

b. Any senior officer in the technical stream, immediately after his promotion to a team/group/departmental head position should undergo a scientifically designed course in administration designed by the HR department. This course should expose him to the relevant administrative jurisprudence so that he understands that any violation by any of his team member/s will also implicate him. In this case, Sangam's boss formulated and endorsed a faulty movement order for which Sangam suffered.

c. Whenever there is a penal provision, there should be provision for appeal. The circumstances under which the violation took place should be thoroughly scrutinized. Any unintentional and innocent violation has to be dealt with softly and discretely so that there is no victimization. In all these cases, the concerned senior whose junior is being penalized, should be given opportunity to defend his junior to clear the air and get innocence established.

CASE STUDY 29

THE VRS BLUES

Mr. G.T. Kumar was at his wit's end. It has started registering in his mind that nuances of electrical engineering and the nitty-gritty of the game of table tennis were far simpler to master than management. A gold medalist and a brilliant electrical engineer in his professional life and a table tennis player representing his state in the national championship in his younger days, Mr. Kumar is now the Executive Director of M/s. Ravenshaw Industries Ltd. He was assigned the onerous responsibility of clearing the Augean stable of pending promotions in the company by the Board of Directors. Strictly speaking, career planning for the executive cadre and their promotion are the job of the HR functionaries, headed by the Director, HRM in the company. But, there were two good reasons why this burden fell on Mr. Kumar's able shoulders. Firstly, the Director, HRM of the company was a new incumbent who migrated from SAIL just three months back and was yet to catch up with the HR challenges the company was facing. Secondly, due to the ad-hoc measures adopted by the management so far, the accumulation of executives at the middle level whose promotion was due, was so enormous, it called for a policy decision.

Authentically, Mr. Kumar has been an operation manager throughout his career. Over and above his solid grip on engineering (after all, his employer company was a high-tech engineering industry), his tremendous dedication, discipline and a cool temperament in the face of acute crises have contributed to his executive capacity. His calm, quiet, just and unperturbed approach has saved the company from quite a few embarrassments in the past. So, it was no wonder that he was elevated to the coveted rank of Executive Director, in –charge of the overall operation of the factory. But, this time, he really seemed totally out of his depth.

It has been a policy of the company to promote an executive duly qualified (i.e. a graduate engineer, ICWA, M-Com, PG Diploma in HRM etc.) once in every four years of uninterrupted service, provided he/she has put up at least an above average contribution to the company. Starting from the Grade I up to the Grade IV, there was no noticeable stagnation as there is no drastic change in the job profile and responsibility. Moreover, there was one more compelling reason for the company to give regular promotion to the younger executives because if they get demotivated, they would quit as their mobility at a young age is far higher. But, stagnation starts at Grades V and VI as at this rank they are required to head a department. The number of new departments is not expanding proportionately with the number of executives available at this rank.

There might be other poignant and even sinister reasons that can be attributed to the phenomenon of overcrowding of promotable executives in these ranks i.e. stagnation. Firstly, a reason can be poignant in the sense that executives go to these ranks in their middle ages after completing about two decades of service. At this age, their mobility is seriously compromised as they are already in their comfort zones professionally, socially and from family considerations. So, there is a sense of helplessness and frustration when there is no advancement in career.

There is even a sinister dimension in this phenomenon in the sense that technological obsolescence compels the company to open new departments sometimes, i.e. not because of expansion of business with the existing technology. It is rather unlikely that an executive in his middle age, who has settled in his comfort zone, will acquire additional qualification, learn new technology so that he becomes eligible to head the new department. Mostly, in these situations, the company has to import specialists from outside thereby further aggravating the situation.

Kumar, with all the wisdom at his command, proposed to the management the introduction of voluntary retirement scheme (VRS) i.e. golden handshake. All the executives who completed twenty years of continuous service in the company could opt for VRS to seek their fortune elsewhere. Their voluntary departure was incentivized depending on the number of years of service left for retirement.

The management, the BoD, had no other choice but to agree for parting with a sizeable and trained, experienced workforce. There was a total disaster as soon as the scheme was announced and introduced. All the brilliant executives, the potential next generation of leaders who could take over the organization in the near future, opted for departure. All those deadwoods that had nowhere to go, stayed back, to inherit the leadership. This is quite apart from the fact the company also bled financially due to heavy cash outflow to pay for the separation, thereby jeopardizing the P/L account, at least for that financial year.

Questions:

i. Was the management right in assigning the job of evolving policy decision pertaining to the HR domain? Could they consider other options more effectively?

Yes, a prudent management could have chosen other options. As the decision to be taken was a policy decision of far reaching consequences, the management should have constituted an expert committee without hesitation to involve outside experts as consultants. The incumbent Director, HR had to be a member of that committee mandatorily. There was, as such, nothing wrong in including Mr. Kumar in the committee in view of his experience, seniority and position in the company.

No doubt, Mr. Kumar had several sterling qualities, but in other areas of management, not in HR and OB that are pertinent here. So, it was imprudent on the part of the management to put the entire responsibility on Mr. Kumar alone. Now, it appears that he lacked wisdom in those in those areas.

ii. Could there be more reasons of stagnation in the Grades V and VI other than those mentioned in this case narration?

Yes, there seem to be reasons also, other than lack of mobility and technological obsolescence. It is the fact that the Grades V and VI are those at the top of the tactical level. The next higher level i.e. Grade VII is the lowest in the strategic level where the responsibility drastically changes. The competence and dexterity demanded in the strategic level are no an extension of those required at the tactical level and are quite different. Tactical level is earmarked with technicalities i.e. evolving processes and methods whereas the strategic level is concerned with evolving policy issues. Many brilliant tactical managers find themselves out of depth in the strategic level and there is heavy screening and rejections. So, because of the lack of the scope of further promotion coupled with the lack of mobility, there is stagnation.

iii. Was Mr. Kumar right in recommending a policy decision of introducing VRS? Could management create some safeguards while introducing the policy measure?

Mr. Kumar was definitely right in introducing VRS when there was heavy stagnation at a particular rank and there was no way to clear the mess otherwise. But, as safeguards, the management should have introduced the scheme with a few safety riders as follow:

a. Management should have reserved the right of its discretion while allowing VRS for a particular executive who has applied for the same. In other words, the management should have reserved the right to screen and scrutinize all the applications for VRS and select only those who could be spared and blocked the passage of those who could not be spared, thereby avoiding the situation of leadership vacuum at the larger overall interest of the company. The management should have consulted legal experts regarding the legal soundness of its discretionary power.

b. The management also should have reserved for itself the right to identify the deadwoods, in its judgment and discretion and ask them to take VRS and leave.

c. VRS, as a strategy of the management was highly merited in view of the fact that executives could seek career opportunities elsewhere instead of stagnating and getting demoralized and frustrated. But, it should not have been done indiscriminately the way it was done.

iv. Could management take some proactive measures to avert the situation turning into a crisis?

Yes, of course. The management could have and should have taken proactive measures to not only foresee the situation developing and also avert it turning into a crisis in the way it did. The answer is again grooming. Every management worth its salt should take pains to identify the potential future leaders and groom them meticulously so as to avoid leadership vacuum in future. Specifically in this case, just before introducing VRS, the identified future leaders should have been called and taken into confidence and briefed regarding the merit of this measure and for whom it is targeted. They also should have been given to understand the prospect that the entire measure was aimed at getting rid of the deadwoods and make the path clear for a smooth take over when the time comes.

v. What HR lessons you learn from this case study?

    a. Any policy decision of serious consequences should not be taken by an individual however brilliant otherwise he is. It should always be entrusted to a committee constituted for the purpose. If the policy is pertaining to HR issue, the Director, HR would have to be included in the committee mandatorily.

    b. Blanket policy measures should be avoided as far as possible. There should be always room for discretion and discrimination.

    c. The management should have created intermediate ranks without higher powers but with higher salary so that a few of the stagnated executives could be promoted without higher responsibility.

MANAGEMENT BY CRISIS AND ITS UNDESIRABLE CONSEQUENCES

Mr. Sudhakar Babu was quite excited. He is the CEO of M/s. Paper Shredder Ltd, a company he has built virtually from scratch. Started as a small proprietary outfit in his own outhouse in Hyderabad, now the company's shares are listed in Hyderabad, Chennai and Kolkata stock exchanges. Babu, a MBA alumnus from Bharatidasan, Trichy, was campus recruited by a renowned MNC. But, within about five years, he felt restless, he was bent upon asserting his own individuality. He quit and established Paper Shredders. Now, after more than a decade, the company was staring at a not so bright future as the whole business world was moving towards paperlessness. Apart from the adverse market condition looming large, there were myriad other internal problems too.

Babu was addressing a meeting of his Board of Directors. He said: "Never allow your people to settle down in their respective comfort zones, that is very dangerous for the company. This company is not only for its employees; we have a host of other stake holders to satisfy. A certain amount of tension and anxiety is necessary to keep people on their toes. Otherwise, they will fall blissfully asleep disregarding all the challenges around."

Other members of the BoD: "You mean to say that there should always be an atmosphere of tension to get the best out of people, but how do you manage to do that?"

– By engineering a crisis and making people aware of that; when there is a shake-up, they will pull up their socks and tighten their belts.

– To achieve what? As of now, our workers and supervisors are performing well; they are meeting their targets and earning handsome bonus, what else you want them to do, by creating an artificial crisis when none really exists?

– That's precisely the problem. They are too complacent and we have allowed them to be so to our own undoing. Remember, when everything seems fine, we are definitely missing something and I have identified that. See, when an average worker is meeting targets happily without straining himself, and earning a handsome bonus, something, somewhere is seriously wrong. I think our performance standards are too loose, our standard times are too large as the allowances are too generous. We have to cut down all these to improve our bottom-line to pull up our EPS, otherwise, we are serving the workers at the cost of the shareholders. How long you can or should do that?

– But, these standards were recommended by industrial engineering experts hired from outside. You mean to say we have to revise them?

– Certainly, but I am not questioning the experts we hired. Our product range is very small; the workers have gathered a huge expertise in their limited range of activities and are earning lavish bonus. We have to curtail all that; we have to tighten our standards.

– Then, we have to take the trade union into confidence before we can set new standards. But, that simply seems impossible.

– Create panic, create a sense of insecurity; all will wake up and fall in line. Just see.

The Board of Directors took their CEO Mr. Babu very seriously as in the meeting nobody opposed him or gave any opinion to the contrary although they were absolutely free to do so. The Director, Operations and the Director, Marketing took the responsibility of spreading the rumour that the company was in a crisis and had to take recourse to downsizing by retrenchment and lay-off. The Director, HR in whose jurisdiction these measures come, felt distinctly uncomfortable but preferred to keep quiet. They used the management appointed grapevine to spread the rumour among the workforce. The labour union got alarmed and confronted the management, how the authorities could retrench and lay-off people without taking the union into confidence? – They demanded.

Management told the union that the company was facing recession and drastic measures like tightening the standards and restricting the incentives were necessary to cut down costs to improve bottom line. The union was not convinced and refused to budge. On the other hand, most of the skilled and highly trained workers and supervisors started quitting in droves to escape job loss and insecurity.

And thereby, the company converted an artificial and imaginary crisis into a real one.

Questions:

i. Was the threat to the company totally artificial or imaginary or real from the beginning?

The threat to the company M/s Paper Shredder Ltd was real from the day one, chiefly because of its marketing myopia. As far as it appears from the narration of this case study, the company was a single product one and that too with an almost obsolete product. It did not bother to diversify and engage its workforce for a new product. When the time study was done to start with at the beginning, the product was new to the workers and the recorded time they took was longer which came down substantially with time and experience. Their productivity was high and they earned handsome bonus which the company could not afford with a shrinking market. Improvement in productivity can help a company only when there is an expanding market.

The company's problems could be ascribed to its management's shortsightedness in product management but the brunt was to be borne by the workers as the management proposed to tighten the performance standards.

ii. Was the CEO's advice sound and reasonable from HRM point of view?

As a CEO, whose job is to look after the interests of all the stake holders without discrimination, he gave a prudent advice keeping in view the overall interests of all the stakeholders. But he targeted only the employees as the main culprit whereas the main challenge was lying somewhere else. His interaction with the other directors brings to light his deep concern for safeguarding the interests of the shareholders by giving them higher EPS which, in turn, could be achieved by not expanding the market but by cutting the labour cost.

Notwithstanding the fact that his proposals and exhortations might have made a lot of sense to the other functionaries but definitely not HR. His measure was anti workers.

iii. How do you justify the CEO's statement that other than the employees, the company had various stakeholders to satisfy? What is the significance of such a statement?

The CEO's statement of the existence of the other stake holders and their concern is very well justified. Starting from the shareholders, the Board of Directors, the executives, the employees, the trade union, the banks/financial institutions, the customers, the suppliers, the government and above all, the society at large, all are the stakeholders in a corporate entity and it is very much the duty of the CEO to do equitable justice to all these stake holders in the sense that no particular stake holder should be unduly pampered at the cost of other stake holder/s.

That was precisely the problem here; the CEO felt that the worker community as a stakeholder was getting unduly pampered at the cost of the shareholder community, which he opposed.

iv. What should have been the duties of the HR Director under the circumstances? Did he do justice to his position?

It appears that the Director, HR was unduly circumspect and withdrew from his role at the behest of the CEO. Thereby, he did not do justice to his role. As a HR expert, he should have foreseen the perils of the measures the management was about to take and warned the BoD beforehand to forestall precipitating the issue.

v. What HR and OB lessons you learn from this case study?

An alert and inquisitive student of HR can learn a few valuable lessons from this case study:

a. Any negotiation with the recognized trade union for evolving mutual agreement pertaining to fixation of standard time, productivity, incentive, bonus etc. through collective bargaining, should have a provision of review after every three years even if there is no change in the product line.

b. Every functional director, as a member of the Board of Directors, should be strong and particular about safeguarding the interests of the people working under his functions in the organization. He should not accept on his shoulders the burden of mistakes or shortcomings of the people in other functional areas. This is a right and privilege which he should not sacrifice at the altar of maintaining peace, cordiality and harmony in the board. He may even go out of the way to safeguard the interests and rights of his people.

c. The HR function of any organization is not only a cost function, it is also a revenue function. Which way it turns out to be depends upon the competence and dexterity of the management.

CASE STUDY 31

WHO CAN BE THE PROJECT MANAGER?

Amitabh Nayak, the CEO of M/s. Cogentrix Conglomerate had a formidable professional challenge in hand. Nayak, in his early fifties now, an alumnus of IIT, Bombay, Mechanical, has been at the helm of affairs of Cogentrix behemoth for about a decade now. A thrust on international business over the years has seen Cogentrix's global footprint growing steadily. They have manufacturing facilities in key geographies and offices and customers in over thirty countries now. Amitabh Nayak is the CEO of the Indian outfit headquartered at Mumbai, of the American MNC.

Cogentrix's Indian chapter has been making heavy machineries for the last about a hundred years much before India opened up its economy to global opportunities in the early nineties in the last century. In reputation, Cogentrix has been synonymous with excellence by virtue of its quality, technology and delivery. It enjoys an ocean of confidence of the customer in whatever it has done so far and it wants to maintain that reputation in whatever it plans to do in the near and distant future. This reputation has also been due to its transparent management practices and a robust organizational culture. It is truly a global company, not only a MNC.

Cogentrix's range of heavy machineries mostly includes earthmovers, excavators, bull-dozers, concrete mixers, types of conveyor buckets for moving earth, soils, minerals or ores. With the current Central government's emphasis on infrastructure, low cost housing for the masses, smart city projects for making fly-overs, laying roads and highways, Cogentrix finds tremendous opportunities for conglomerate diversification in the area of projects. But, everything said and done, projects are different from products and hence, project management is also a lot different from production management. Mr. Nayak's intuition was dictating him that the company would hit the bull's eye of rapid expansion if it goes for turn key projects in the areas of construction and mining.

Moreover, Nayak's gut feeling was not allowing him to limit the company's foray into hardware only. Managing huge infrastructure projects running into several hundred crores of Rupees, will definitely require highly versatile software application supports. Who would develop those software requiring expert domain knowledge which will be available with the company in the near future? But then, managing hardware projects involving the so-called brick and mortar is quite different from managing software projects and Mr. Nayak was well aware of that. So, to summarize, Mr. Nayak had three challenges in hand: convincing the BoD for venturing into projects from traditional production, finding a suitable head for the infrastructure project and another head for the software projects.

Now, who could be a project manager? What should be his qualification, experience and capabilities? How these qualities would be different for brick and mortar projects and software projects? He was wondering. Should he be an insider with proven abilities or an outside expert who could be tried to fit in the company at a senior level? These were the questions confronting him. As of now, he had three insiders in his mind all in their mid-forties and middle management level. One was a production manager with a BE in mechanical plus MBA in Operations, a brilliant Chartered Accountant who was a finance manager and a HR manager who was a B-Com with MBA plus LLB. What if he could be an expert from outside who ultimately prove to be a misfit with the company's culture? He felt it was too risky for him to take such vital decision alone i.e all by himself. He was wondering whether it would be appropriate on his part to advise his company secretary to call for a BoD meeting to discuss this issue to arrive at a consensus.

Questions:

i. What is "conglomerate diversification?" What are the HR challenges associated with it?

When an organization goes for producing goods and offering services in totally unrelated areas, the organization is said to have undertaken a conglomerate diversification. One of the best examples of conglomerate diversification is that of M/s. ITC Ltd, which started with cigarettes and its constituent elements like tobacco and filters and diversified into totally unrelated areas like running hotels together with making a line of agro – based products and food products plus exercise books for students.

Conglomerate diversification is a very challenging strategic move by the management. The positive side of this strategy is that it is a deft and bold move by which the management can leverage its leadership status in one existing product line into a new product line. The challenge lies in the fact that due to lack of familiarity, its expertise, particularly in operation and HR areas, will fall short of the requirements.

In HR areas, the challenge is even more serious. When the company needs fresh blood and leadership in keeping with its name in operation areas, HR has to identify, locate and procure them. Placements of these newly inducted manpower into appropriate positions among the existing man power and ensuring their mutual co-operation is a real challenge.

ii. How project management is different from production management?

In operation management, we encounter both project management and production management. These two distinct areas of operation management differ from each other in many respects. In an organization, production is a routine and regular activity and all the units of the same product are made identical to each other, as far as possible, intentionally. Any lack of similarity between two units of the same product is unintentional, accidental, undesirable and by default. Products are intentionally made different from each other only when they are custom built i.e. to suit a particular customer's requirement. A product can be very tiny to very big.

On the other hand, a project is a bigger entity which is always custom built and is unique to suit the customer. No two projects are exactly identical. Projects involve non-repetitive and intermittent activities. Every project has a well defined starting and ending points. In fact, a project precedes production.

For example, establishing/setting up a factory is a project and then the production commences. Similarly, an airport has to be constructed and commissioned before the air travel services can commence. A project, quite unlike production, requires involvement of experts in different disciplines intensely working together to complete it within time and budgeted cost. All these experts work under a project manager for a specified duration. Because of these, project management is a very challenging task.

iii. How hardware projects are different from software projects?

This question can be answered from our understanding of the differences between hardware and software. Hardware involve hard entities in the real world but software involves soft entities in the virtual world. Hardware, once made wrongly, can't be altered or modified easily and may have to be abandoned or rejected which can make the process very costly. Software inaccuracies or mistakes, once detected, can be corrected easily by screen based editing. As application software are mostly custom built, they undergo heavy alteration and modification during their development which is virtually impossible for hardware. So, hardware projects, when custom built, have to be executed very cautiously. That makes a hardware project very challenging for the project manager.

Both hardware and software projects call for involvement of experts from diverse fields. Software involve domain experts in various business process areas and program writers to develop the logic, whereas hardware involves experts in different branches of engineering i.e. mechanical, electrical, civil, electronics, computer science, architecture etc. Both hardware and software projects are time and cost bound.

iv. What are the qualities of a project manager? How these qualities can be different for hardware and software projects?

The two top most qualities of a project manager are versatility and emotional maturity. Otherwise, the qualities of a project manager can be briefly enumerated as:

    a. Strong technical background

    b. Mature and accomplished individual

    c. Currently available with good terms with the other senior executives

    d. Can keep the project team happy and together

    e. Versatile experience and capability

Over and above these, to be a successful project manager, he is expected to have certain special qualities:

    a. Credibility

    b. Sensitivity

    c. Leadership and management style

    d. Ability to handle stress

The qualities required for a project manager for hardware and software projects are not very different. Software project mangers are expected to have a few additional qualities because of the very nature of software product:

    a. Liaising ability among the customer, domain expert and program writer

    b. Spokesperson on behalf of the team to the management

    c. Ability to put up longer hours when the project is nearing completion

    d. Sound judgment as to when the first prototype should be delivered to the customer.

For a hardware project, delivering the first prototype for subsequent iterative modifications does not arise.

    v. What are the HR & OB challenges in project management?

        First and foremost, the organization structure for project management should be different from that required for regular production management. Project management organization structure is a modified version of matrix structure i.e. a basic matrix structure in which suitable modification is introduced to cater to the different kinds of projects.

As is well known, the principal HR challenge in a matrix organization is violation of the principle of 'Unity of Command" of Henry Fayol. In a matrix structure, a functionary has to report to two bosses i.e. one line and one staff. The staff boss is for expert advice and the line boss is for command and execution. Sometimes, there may be contrasting instruction/command from the two different bosses and the functionary caught up in between will be confused as to whom to follow.

Moreover, for performance rating, a functionary may be rated highly by one boss but quite lowly by another boss. The concerned HR manager will be confused to decide which rating is correct. On the other hand, as far as OB challenges are concerned, there are mainly two to guard against:

a. When experts in diverse fields of profession come together and contribute for the progress and success of the project, ego clashes are inevitable. As is the nature of human beings, a professional who is a recognized expert in his field, will mostly tend to think that his own field is the most important and the other professionals are sub-ordinate. Ironically, each professional thinks the same and it becomes extremely difficult for the project manager to keep them together till the end of the project.

b. The second challenge is called "projectitis." When a group of people work together for a specified duration for a project, they undergo four phases of relationship i.e. forming, storming, norming and performing. After the project team is formed, there will be clashes to be settled and adjudicated by the project manager who would set the norms. During the performance phase, the members develop emotional bonds with one another which normally outlast the project. When the project gets over, the attachment suddenly gets snapped which acts as an emotional shock to the members, hard to overcome. The organizational OB experts have to take recourse to counseling to overcome this.

vi. Should the CEO promote an insider or bring in an outsider? What would be the respective HR and OB challenges in each case?

As per the narration of the case, there are three identified contenders for the post of project manager from inside. If one is promoted, the other two will have to be suitably looked after, otherwise they will be demoralized. If someone is brought from outside, all these three will be demoralized. Moreover, when an expert from outside is brought in as the project boss, he may not get the requisite co-operation from the existing insiders and he may find it difficult to function.

In this case, it appears that, as per the quality requirements for a project manager, the mechanical engineer is the most suitable for the hardware projects. Of course, he has to be trained in project management from a renowned professional institute. An outsider has to be brought in for the software projects.

vii. Is the BoD the right forum to decide on this issue? Should the CEO call for a BOD meeting to discuss this issue?

The BOD is definitely the right forum to discuss the issue of the company's foray into project management but may not be the right forum to take a final decision on the issue of appointing a project manager. The BOD, after a thorough discussion, should form an expert committee which should go into every aspect of this issue and take a decision.

For the BOD to meet, the CEO should call for a meeting.

CASE STUDY 32

ATTITUDE, APTITUDE, ALTITUDE AND ALL THAT

Mr. Simranjit Singh Alhuwalia, in his early fifties, has been an astute observer of human behavior for the last about thirty years of his career in the banking industry. A gold medalist and a first rank holder in his graduation in commerce from Delhi University, he joined the biggest public sector bank in India i.e. the State bank of India as a probationary officer during the pre-liberalization era. Since then, he has taken his life and career very seriously and sincerely. In the course of his career, he has developed a conviction that "It is far better to deserve than desire – if we deserve, even then we may not get something but it would be better than getting something without deserving. Dignity lies in deserving whether we get something or not."

True to his conviction, he completed his CAIIB meticulously, although he has been witnessing with consternation that a few of his colleagues were getting promotion without ever bothering about acquiring any such professional qualification. All those high flying whiz-kids, nevertheless, had one thing in common. They all had a very pleasing personality disposition, he observed. All those smart guys were busy in building up relationships with their bosses and colleagues wherever they were posted, rather than building up themselves. Mr. Singh chose otherwise, he relied on himself more than being pleasing for others. He built himself up, brick by brick, professionally to become an asset for the bank making a good deal of personal sacrifice, but, in the bargain, was labelled 'self – centered' – he recollects ruefully.

Their employer, SBI, however, did not gain anything by promoting those pleasing guys. All of them left for greener pastures, post bank liberalization, with three times hike in salaries. It was not that Singh was not lured with such offers, when there was explosive expansion in the banking sector and private sector giants came into picture, but Singh did not desert his public sector employer. His disdain for those giant private sector banks offering dream salaries to take away executives at the upper middle levels in the public sector had one more reason. He believed that these attitude mongers flourish more in those private behemoths who traditionally had scanty regards for professional qualification.

Singh's regard and devotion to public sector did not go unrewarded, though. He became GM, duly that too, by overtaking a few seniors I. e. his extraordinary sense of discipline and dedication were noticed. His salary was high but earthly, not heavenly like his private sector counterparts. So, he felt, kind of, let down by destiny. In his own home ground, by quirk of fate, so to say, he had to report to an Executive Director who happened to be a lady with a plain engineering degree without any banking professional qualification like CAIIB. He has no grievance about the gender, but the position? "It is a gross injustice – who is more knowledgeable in banking? – he laments.

Simranjeet recollects once he was deputed by SBI for a MDP for middle managers conducted by MDI, Gurgaon a few years back. There, the trainer who was known to be an HR expert, was talking about the resounding triumvirate i.e. attitude, aptitude and altitude, which, however, at that point of time, was beyond his comprehension.

How can a senior officer be allowed to come up further and occupy key positions by mongering attitude only without acquiring the requisite expertise which is reflected in his prestigious professional qualifications? What is attitude after all? How can attitude be preferred and rewarded overriding aptitude in a particular profession? Who is more useful to the organization as a whole, the person with the right aptitude or one with the right attitude? Can attitude contribute to competence? Can attitude compensate for the lack of requisite competence?

Can you promote somebody incessantly just because he has a pleasing personality and you like him ignoring his professional shortcomings? Will it not be harmful for the whole organization? He wonders. These were the intriguing questions tormenting him for quite some time. At times, he mulls over taking voluntary retirement.

There were quite a few private training institutes in Delhi imparting advanced professional training in banking and he could join any one of them. They would, at least, recognize his special talent and pay him adequately and moreover, it would be a valuable service to the society – he believed.

Questions:

i. What is attitude? How can it contribute to an executive's professional advancement?

The literal meaning of attitude according to the dictionary is "A mental predisposition or a settled/stable way of thinking or feeling about something or a tendency to respond positively or negatively towards a certain idea, object, person or situation. It influences an individual's choice of action and response to challenges, incentives, rewards i.e. stimulation."

To a managerial task or an issue, the concerned manager's mental disposition can be positive, negative or even neutral which is very rare and exceptional. Simply speaking, if the attitude is positive towards the task, the manager will devote himself to do it, but if his competence for the job does not permit, he won't be able to do it in spite of having willingness.

On the other hand, if his attitude is negative, in spite of his competence, he won't take up the job and his competence would go waste. Mostly, it is seen that when there is a strong motivation on the part of the manager, he would cover up his lack of competence, if any, by his will power along the way. In common parlance, attitude is reflected in a functionary's interpersonal behavioral skills. His personal professional skill may be lacking in a particular area, but because of his favourable relationships which he builds up, he gets co-operation from others and thereby covers up his shortcomings and move ahead.

ii. What is aptitude? Can't it be gained or promoted? How? What are the benefits of the organization in promoting aptitude?

Aptitude is a term used to signify any special ability or knack of an individual in doing something i.e. in some specific area of activity. It is a capability either innate or acquired, in some professional area. From the very definition itself, it is obvious that aptitude can be gained or promoted, provided, of course, it is identified correctly. Each of us has been born with some special capability of doing something well inherently. If that capability and the area of activity is identified in time, we can be experts in our respective areas by virtue of proper training and development. It is believed in HR that the potential of development of humans in the correctly identified niche area is virtually infinite.

The corresponding rewards and benefits for the employer organization is also immense. It is a win-win situation for both the employer and the employee. It is the job of the HR functionaries to identify the niche areas of aptitude of people under their jurisdiction and build them up by well – designed extensive training. In an organization, if the concerned HR functionaries are strong and committed in this area, the employees will be more motivated and productive owing to job satisfaction and the employer will gain by higher engagement, productivity, lesser employee turnover and higher profitability.

iii. How aptitude and attitude are different? Which would be more important and useful for an individual and an organization?

Both these terms i.e. attitude and aptitude have been defined earlier in the answers to the previous questions. To repeat, aptitude is the name of a special inclination or inherent ability or knack in doing something. Attitude is mental disposition towards a particular job or task in organizational context. It can be positive, negative or neutral. Neutral attitudes are also termed indifferent attitude. Both neutral and negative attitudes are harmful for an organization.

Obviously, it is a matter of common sense to figure out that aptitude and attitude are related to each other. In the areas of our aptitude, our attitude will be positive as we derive satisfaction and fulfillment from those areas. To the contrary, if we are forced to work in those areas where we don't have aptitude, our attitude may be negative and hence, our performance sub-optimal.

It is commonly believed that, in organizational context, attitude is more important than aptitude. If we can develop positive attitude, by attitudinal training, in a number of areas of activity, we need not be particular about the niche areas of our aptitude and contribute to the other areas and thereby broadband our aptitude itself. It will also immensely benefit the employer organization.

iv. Was Mr. Singh right in his thinking and conviction? Was his strong conviction useful for himself and his employer?

Of course, Mr. Singh's thinking and conviction were right provided they could be interpreted in the right perspective. Let us explain. Mr. Singh was not against attitude per se neither he underestimated or undermined the importance of right attitude to the employer organization. His bitterness was precisely regarding attitude mongering i.e. taking undue advantage of having pleasing personality and thereby misleading the higher ups in believing that the person concerned has the right attitude.

He observed that the higher ups had undue soft corner for pleasing personalities; their shortcomings were overlooked and they used to get rewarded out of the way. So, those pleasing personalities were exploiting this weakness to the hilt and were coming up in an easier way without bothering to acquire the right qualification for the job or position. In other words, altitude was acquired by misusing attitude and at the cost of aptitude.

Mr. Singh's strong conviction was definitely useful for both himself and his employer. But, unfortunately, he did not get the recognition he deserved. His strong conviction to develop himself so that he could be more useful to the employer, was misinterpreted as wrong attitude.

v. Is there any justification in thinking that the private sector values attitude higher than the public sector? If so, is there any underlying reason for the same?

Yes, indeed. Private sector is mostly driven by result and positive attitude seems to deliver result. The sector is less concerned with somebody's qualification and more concerned with qualities of producing results.

On the other hand, public sector follows certain well-defined norms which consider qualification and experience and in the bargain sometimes actual result gets lesser attention. They strictly abide by rules and regulations which are made not only around results but also qualification and seniority.

vi. What are the HR and OB lessons you learn from this case study?

For an astute reader, one can learn several hard lessons from this case study:

HR:

a. Practitioners in this field in the organization should be watchful enough to identify who is genuinely useful for the organization and who is faking it for their own selfish gains. People should not be allowed to sail through by using pleasing manners and behavior alone. They should be told point blank that pleasing manners and display of positive attitude is no substitute for professional qualification/s. Positive attitudes are desirable and can complement professional qualification but can't replace it.

b. There should be concrete and unambiguous, well defined norms for promotion. These norms should not be vague and should have distinct weightage for professional qualification/s. Otherwise, smart people will take undue advantage of it.

c. It is incumbent upon the HR functionaries to locate and identify the genuinely sincere, serious and dedicated employees and take due care of them. They should not be made to feel left out and uncared for just because they are not very popular. Popularity is no substitute for competence and sincerity.

OB:

a. Genuinely sincere people are the real assets of the company. They may not be always loud and visible. They may not always blow their own trumpets. Their silence is not their weakness. Their contribution and sincerity should speak for themselves and that message should be understood.

b. If altitude is given to people with attitude ignoring aptitude, sub-optimal performance will be the norms rather than exception in the organization. Persons with correct attitude should be told to acquire the correct aptitude and conversely, persons with the right aptitude should be trained to cultivate the right attitude. Then only, both attitude and aptitude will work together to gain altitude.

CASE STUDY 33

INTRIGUES OF ORGANIZATION DESIGN

Mr. Arvind Bhatnagar has a problem at hand. A post graduate in economics with a MSW from Jaipur, he is the Director, HRD of M/s Pallavi Electric Ltd, a listed company in the Bombay stock exchange, having their main factory at Noida, western UP and their corporate office in Delhi, NCR. Established by a technocrat entrepreneur about a couple of decades back, Pallavi is a familiar name in the electronic and electrical hardware industry for quality and technology. The company makes a wide range of electronic and electrical switches, relays, speed regulators, dimers etc., and has been a regular and reliable OEM supplier for giant electrical and electronic, particularly power electronic industries in India and abroad. Control panel components and accessories for power plants and other applications are their forte.

Pallavi products are designed with innovative ideas keeping in mind product performance, reliability, safety and customer delight. All the products are designed and developed mostly in-house using very versatile and appropriate application software and are manufactured using state of the art technology, equipment and materials. With over twenty years of experience in the industry, Pallavi demonstrates the ability to be innovative and responsive to rapid changes in lifestyle and market place. Pallavi's edge in the market is its unrivalled breadth of technical solutions for all product groups and customer business situations.

For all these supremacies in product innovation and marketing, the strength and backbone for the company has been its human resources and Arvind Bhatnagar is duly proud of that. With its skilled, dedicated and disciplined workforce,

Pallavi aspires to explore new horizons, hitherto quite uncharted areas as far as the company's activities are concerned. Just that day, Subhash Agarwal, the company's founder CEO (an alumnus of IIT, Delhi) called Arvind in his chamber:

Subhash: Arvind, I wish to tell you something very important. Indeed, I have a challenge for you. Are you ready?

Arvind: Yes, of course. But, what is it? Let me know.

Subhash: The other day, I was going through the account statement of the company to be filed to the ROC. I found we are spending a fortune in buying software to manage our design process and distribution. I think, it is high time that we ourselves start developing application software for captive consumption i.e. use in house and save a good lot of money. When the operating margin improves, I know how to make both the workforce and the shareholders a lot happier. Why can't you ponder over this? It would be a tremendous HR challenge for you, I suppose.

Arvind: Do you want me to make a proposal?

Subhash: Precisely. But, not only you, sit with the other Directors with the Company Secretary. It will have ramifications in all the functional areas but your function will be the most impacted. That is why I am asking you to co-ordinate the whole issue.

Arvind could not counter his CEO on his face, but he was not exactly convinced. When you foray into an altogether new area of activity, why it should be a HR challenge only? He was wondering. For the first time in his career, he felt out of depth. "All the problems of the company are dumped on my head." – he was grumbling. He felt he was a victim, all the good thigs he does, he rarely gets accolades but any mistake or shortcoming are highlighted and amplified. Nevertheless, he organized a meeting of all the functional directors and the company secretary. The meeting, however, was tantamount to opening the proverbial Pandora's box:

Company Secretary: First of all, let us decide whether the software activity will be done in a new division or a new subsidiary to be floated now. Our existing

MOA does not have provision for software. We have to either amend it or go for a new one.

Director, Finance: The capital structure for a software company should be different from that of a hardware company. A new division will not involve a new capital structure, a new company will. But, will you have the requisite man power to call for a new company?

Director, Marketing: When our company is going to make a new product, whether software or hardware, meant only for captive consumption, where is the marketing challenge involved? I have been called in this meeting unnecessarily.

Director, Information Systems: Out of all the functional areas, the activity will be directly relevant to my domain, my responsibility is going to multiply three times. I don't mind, provided you compensate me for it adequately; what about that, Mr. Director HR? He, sort of, challenged.

Director, Operations: I am confident quite a few of my people can be trained in the new area instead of bringing in freshers from outside. That will reduce cost also, but I shall require replenishment.

Arvind felt quite overwhelmed by these reactions. He decided to raise the level i.e. put the ball back to the CEO's court, after all, the idea was his brain child.

Questions:

i. What can be the difference between a problem and a challenge? Why Arvind felt that the task assigned to him was more of a problem rather than a challenge?

It is worth finding the difference only when the two things have certain similarities. It does not make much of a sense when we try to differentiate between chalk and cheese because they are two diverse things without any similarity.

What are the similarities between a problem and a challenge? In common parlance, both have negative connotations. Both pose threats to our progress, our objectives and sometimes, even to our existence.

Loosely, these two terms are used as synonyms i.e. meaning the same thing. But, there are subtle differences worth exploring particularly in management science.

There is one school of thought which says that negative connotations should not be ascribed to both these terms. It is all a matter of perception by the person who is subject to either problem or threat. According to the taker's perception, problems have negative whereas challenges have positive connotations. In other words, a threatening issue can seem to be a problem when we have a negative attitude toward it and a challenge when our attitude toward it is positive.

This school of thought can be further rationalized a bit more objectively. Every threatening issue have two contrasting aspects, one is a punitive, task or cost aspect another is the reward or pay-off aspect. That is why it is said that every opportunity has a challenge and every challenge an opportunity. Both the problem and the challenge have to be won over or overcome.

In this course of overcoming or meeting the problem or the challenge, we incur cost, undergo punishment, complete tasks, spend resources, make sacrifices etc, and when we successfully meet the challenge or overcome the problem, we get rewarded or paid off. Now, the line of distinction precisely is, when the rewards are less than the cost, the issue is perceived as a problem; on the contrary, when the rewards are more than the sacrifices involved, the issue is perceived as a challenge.

That is why challenges are viewed as potential opportunities whereas problems remain in the realm of dangers. Then a pertinent question arises. If the rewards are less than the cost, why we should confront a problem at the first place? The answer is, we don't confront problems voluntarily, they are thrust upon us by the forces of circumstances. Challenges, at least sometimes, are taken up voluntarily as we perceive potential opportunities in them in the form of higher rewards.

ii. Do you subscribe to the view expressed by the finance director that the capital structures for hardware and software companies should be different? Why?

Yes, it makes quite a bit of sense when we say that ideal or appropriate capital structure for hardware and software companies should be different simply because the process of wealth creation in these two kinds of entities are at variance. In manufacturing companies, wealth is created by using the infrastructure whereas in the IT companies, it is by using knowledge. Software is a knowledge product.

The infrastructure needed in manufacturing companies are plant and machinery and other supporting physical facilities i.e. tangible assets procured by using long term capital. On the contrary, software is produced by using intellectual or knowledge assets which are intangible provided by the human resources employed in the company. So, software companies need more working capital for salary payments.

The sum and substance of this foregoing discussion implies that in the manufacturing companies, capital structure will be dominated by the debt component so the debt to equity ratio will be high, and this debt will be obtained by hypothecating the tangible assets. In the IT industries, the whole capital may be only equity or minor debt component due to the absence of assets which can be hypothecated. The capital will be dominated by working capital.

iii. As the issue is multi – dimensional, was the CEO right in assigning the task to the Director, HR?

The CEO was fully aware that the issue was multi – dimensional and it was also inappropriate to give the responsibility of conducting the BOD meeting to the Director, HR. But, it was well thought out strategic plan by the CEO. The CEO could guess, from his experience in handling people, that the proposal would ruffle many feathers and upset many apple carts. But, ironically, if he would have chaired the meeting himself, people would have been restrained in coming out with their actual misgivings openly due to the gravity of the CEO's rank. By making the Director, HR conduct the meeting, he made the other Directors come out in the open with their doubts and got the feed back from the Director, HR and could estimate the authenticity of the situation. This strategy enabled him to take the necessary corrective measures.

iv. What are the HR challenges when we go for a new division or a new subsidiary company?

A company feels the necessity of opening a new division under two circumstances, one is expansion with closely related products and the other is venturing into a new product area. The second situation, in turn, can be addressed in two ways, one is opening a new division and the other is opening a new subsidiary. Here, we are addressing the second situation i.e a new product area. In this situation, the principal challenge is in the area of operation as the company has been hitherto a product manufacturer in the domain of hardware, and now venturing into project management in the domain of software. A software is both a product and a project. The HR challenges are concomitant with the challenges in operation management.

It is unlikely that for a hardware manufacturing company, there would be inhouse expertise in developing software. So, for opening a new division, a divisional head has to be identified who can't be promoted from inside the company for the purpose, owing to lack of the requisite expertise. A professional has to be identified outside and inducted in the company as a divisional head. But there will be contentious issues.

The first issue would be regarding culture, the new incumbent should be a match with the company's culture. The second issue is remuneration. Software companies traditionally pay higher, but a new incumbent with a salary more than what fits the company's existing pay structure will only create widespread heartburn among the insiders. To avoid these problematic issues, it is better to have a new subsidiary.

v. What could be the potential OB challenges in the whole issue?

The idea regarding the potential OB challenges can, as well, be gathered from the exchanges and conversations in the Board of Directors' meeting organized by the Director, HR as per the directives of the CEO. The reactions expressed reflect their behavioral issues. Everybody's interest is disturbed or threatened because of the proposed new venture. Every functionary is concerned with his own interest ignoring the interest of the organization as a whole.

In general, whenever there is expansion, people's expectations also get expanded. They hope for raise in status or salary or both. A few of them will get to man the expansion but more number of people will not get. They will get demoralized and that will affect the company's performance adversely for sometime to come.

CASE STUDY 34

WORK-LIFE BALANCE/WORK FROM HOME BLUES

Chanchal and Vidya Doshi make a fine couple. Both of them are techies hailing from Ahmedabad, but have recently settled in Bangalore, the IT capital of India. Chanchal, in his early thirties, is a graduate in Computer Science whereas Vidya, in her late twenties, is a Master of Computer Application (MCA). Both of them are from educated, cultured and upper middle class Gujarati Brahmin families with a strong value system. They have a son, Abheek, who is just five years old. Chanchal and Vidya have got him admitted in an international school located just about five kilometres away from the locality where the couple stays. And that is posing some problems. This is the nearest international school of some reputable standard the couple could find.

Looking back, the primary reason why they migrated from one state capital to the other, down south, is that both of them could find employment in the same software company of mid – size operating in the area of their specialization i.e. their comfort zone. The company, now mid-size, has a good growth prospect in future and the salary, though not that heavenly like a few other IT giant companies in the same city, was reasonable. They never felt socially or culturally alienated because Bangalore has a highly cosmopolitan culture. What is mainly bothering them is the cost of living which is exorbitant compared to that in Ahmedabad.

Not only real estate cost and rentals which are just double, all the other services are incomparably costly –at least that is what the couple feels. That compels both the husband and wife to be professionally engaged and contribute to the family income almost equally. One salary was not enough; only two salaries can make both ends meet. But, Vidya is finding managing professional, social and family life together well neigh impossible. Chanchal contemplates bringing some elderly relative from their home town to Bangalore who would always stay at home to attend to the maid servant and cook as and when they come, escort Abheek to the school van in the morning and receive him back in the evening etc. But, no such elderly person, known or related to Chanchal was ready to come and stay with the couple leaving native place mainly for the fear of unknown language and culture. As this elderly person has to stay back at home to interact with the maid servant and cook, familiarity with the local language is essential.

In this regard, as far as the facilities available with their employer is concerned, there is no such availability as the number of ladies working in the establishment is too small to mandate a crèche, a day care or baby – sitting facilities. Under the circumstances, Vidya believes if she is given a 'work from home' facility/provision so that she can log-in and attend to her job on-line instead of physically being present in the office, she should be able to manage this balancing act. She discusses this idea with her husband and gets the requisite support. She is planning to make an appeal to the management one of these days to introduce this facility especially for ladies having a family with a young child to manage. The management has to take a policy decision to introduce and implement this additional facility for their deserving employees.

Questions:

i. What is the current mandate from the government, as far as crèche facilities in the work place is concerned?

  As per the relevant factories Act 1948, the current mandate is:

  a. Where more than thirty women workers are employed, crèches shall be provided for use of children under the age of six years.

  b. Such physical facility shall provide adequate accommodation, sufficiently lighted and ventilated, maintained in a clean and sanitary condition.

  As per the judgement of the Mumbai High Court in July 2012, software firms come under the purview of the Factories Act, 1948.

ii. What can be the employer's attitude and stand point towards this policy?

The stand point of the management regarding this issue will depend on the attitudinal disposition of the management. An enlightened management with a futuristic outlook should not have hesitation or objection in providing this facility which is not exactly mandated due to the small number of women workers in the workplace, as of now.

For software companies both men and women can contribute equally. For the employer, a woman employee should be preferable in the sense that they are less mobile and more stable and disciplined compared to men. The crèche facility would definitely attract more women who require this facility, when the company goes for future expansion.

But, for a short sighted management, providing this facility calls for immediate expenses without any accompanying return. Management with a conservative outlook may not agree for this. On the other hand, work from home facility can be for both men and women and many IT companies including the renowned MNCs have this facility. In most of the companies, this facility is provided on an ad-hoc basis, depending upon exigencies of circumstances, with prior permission. Providing this facility on a long term basis to a few select employees on merit, may have serious repercussions and implications.

iii. What can be the attitude and standpoints of those employees who are not to be benefited by this policy?

Employees who are not going to get any benefit when management takes a policy decision of introducing facilities like crèche, day-care or playschool etc, can be anyone or more of the following:

a. Total indifference or not bothered attitude i.e. the other employees may feel that the new policy does not affect them in any way and hence, they need not take any interest in it other than idle curiosity. Of course, such indifferent employees will be comparatively less in number.

b. Passively envious, that the management is yielding to the demands of a few employees now. May be in the past, majority of the employees also had young children but neither such facility was demanded nor given. This envy is residing in their psyche, not manifested in terms of any action in the outer world. This category of employees will be majority in number.

c. Actively envious, i.e. their envy is not dormant but finds expression in terms of demands for similar facility in some other area useful for them, so as to balance the scale. Management may be hard put to provide the same; otherwise a portion of the workforce would be demoralized.

The above is for the physical facility of crèches and the like. The repercussion on the employees who won't get work from home facility may be even more serious. They will think that everyone has some issue or the other at home, why favouring only a few? Management would be hard put to extinguish this fire.

iv. What can be the HR and OB challenges inherent in this policy?

The answers to the previous questions, by and large, address this issue. The issue can be considered two folds i.e. physical facility of crèche and work from home. Both these measures have OB implications whereas the later has tremendous HR implications. For work from home, time records and wage/salary calculation will be a stupendous task. For white collar worker that is what Vidya is, salary calculation and performance evaluation will be based on tasks accomplished rather than hours of attendance recorded. Any arrangement for work from home to be effective, it will have to be strictly supervised by the immediate boss in terms of output generated by working possibly throughout the day with gaps in between. The work can't be limited to the otherwise normal working hours.

The OB challenges will be mostly concerned with combating the prevailing sense of inequities and favouritism as explained earlier.

v. What are the pros and cons of husband and wife working in the same organization from both the employee and the employer's point of view?

With the advent of the phenomenon of women joining the workforce in this country more and more, this HR and OB issue has been very pertinent. The pros and cons can be summarized as:

Ads:

    a.   For employees, commuting to the workplace from home would be cheaper as the couple can travel together. If one excels in the profession, the other will try to follow suit. If one is motivated or encouraged, the other won't lag behind, will try to catch up. Any advanced training received by one, will also build up the other.

    b.   For employer, there may be economy in terms of one HRA for the same house address for both husband and wife. Disseminating information and communication will be facilitated, of course, for informal communication. If work from home is allowed for the wife, the husband won't grudge it, other men may. When both the spouses try to out-excel each other, in the bargain, the employer will be benefited.

Dis-ads:

The disadvantages can be very sinister at times like the following:

    a.   For employees, both husband and wife may enter into a bitter rivalry for career progress and that may rock the marriage. If one gets a promotion, the other will get envious; one may look down upon the other. Both these situations will create dis-harmony in the marriage.

    b.   b) For employer, if one is punished, the other may get demoralized. If one is transferred or promoted, the other will demand the same.

CASE STUDY 35

EXPERIENCING ALL THE FOUR 'T'S OF HRM IN AN ILLUMINATED CAREER

Ashok Mitra, Jaya Mitra's father is celebrating his seventy fifth birth anniversary and has invited his daughter, Jaya, along with her family, to attend the celebration and grace the occasion. Ashok is rightly proud of the success and achievement in career of his only child who is currently the GM –HR in a mid-sized software firm in Bangalore. "But those days were quite different" – Ashok reminisces. His nostalgia takes him back by about thirty years when Jaya was hardly fourteen and struggling in her school. Ashok, a post graduate alumnus of NIT, Durgapur (REC in those days) was one of the senior metallurgists of HAL at its head office in Bangalore. He wanted Jaya also to study engineering like him but that was not to be. Jaya was dead scared of mathematics and science and had developed a kind of aversion for those subjects. Ashok was crestfallen, what kind of career success was waiting for a girl who could not study math and science? He wondered.

Ashok, on the advice of one of his colleagues, sought the help of a professional career counselor who sat with Jaya for a good couple of hours interviewing her and at the end advised accompanying Ashok not to impose math and science on her. "Let her choose subjects on humanities and complete her graduation. After that, let her do Master of Social Work (MSW) from a good institution. Don't worry, she would flourish in her career." – He declared. Ashok did exactly that and 'lo and behold' –she has made a success of her in HRM. A software start-up in the mid-eighties recruited her; the company has been successful and so has Jaya. She has stuck to and grown along with the company.

During her hitherto successful career, she has experienced all the four T – s, has fulfilled all the four roles in HRM as classified by Kossek and Block i.e. Transaction, Translation, Transition and Transformation. Immediately after her recruitment and induction, Jaya was sent for an intensive training program to XLRI, Jamshedpur, for as long as six months and she learnt many nuances of HRM. When she came back from training, and started her career as a HR officer, her job was mostly transactional i.e. routine Personnel and IR functions, covering mostly administrative activities such as documenting operational processes and maintaining employee records etc. She mastered the functions within a few years and got promoted to Asst. Manager, HR.

In this rank, her job was mostly translational, she was more of a communicator in which her role was associated with listening and responding to employees and customers' concerns as well as explaining and implementing the policies established by the top management to the employees. She was, kind of, basking in the glory of discharging such responsibilities. In her next incarnation, i.e. next promotion as HR – Manager, her role changed to more of transition. She migrated from HRM to HRD when the organizational processes were realigned to support customer and market demand with a future orientation. Also, this transitional role was concerned with execution of human resources activities, policies and best practices, making all necessary on going changes to support or improve the company's business operational and strategic objectives.

Today, she is the GM-HRD and her role is transformational. This role expands the traditional role of HR into those areas of management where it becomes a challenging exercise to develop business interest and growth. The aim is to turn HRM into a force that can help an organization reach its objectives and instill those objective orientations in the employees. This enables the HR professionals to create values for the organization as a whole. Her role is mostly to do with strategic human resources management.

Questions:

i.   If you have understood exactly the transaction role of a HR professional, give five examples over and above those mentioned in this case.

Transaction role of a HR professional is the usual and conventional 'Personal and Industrial Relation' function. All the so called conventional and traditional roles like recruitment, screening and short listing, conducting test and personal interviews of the short listed candidates, issuing appointment letters, giving induction training to the new recruits, posting them appropriately, monitoring and evaluating their progress, promotion, fresh posting after promotion, transfer, if any, are all transactional roles.

ii. Can the Transaction and Translation roles be categorized into one and Transition and Transformation into another? Elaborate.

The answer to this question is a conservative yes. It is indeed a fact that the functions of transaction and translation have commonalities more than differences, but combining them at the ground level may not be a prudent practice in a complex, multilevel organization. It goes without saying that these two functions we are discussing about, complement each other. Translation facilitates transaction.

HR role, in some ways, is that of interpretation and intermediation between the management and the workforce. A HR functionary is a spokesperson on behalf of management to the work force and vice versa. There may be a sudden flare up in industrial relation and harmony if there is a shortcoming in playing this role. Both transaction and translation are rather routine exercises on which smooth day to day operation depends.

On the other hand, transition and transformation are creative, intermittent roles and, of course, they do complement each other. A run of the mill employee undergoes a transition from a taker to a giver by virtue of this role played dedicatedly and sincerely by the HR manager concerned. A transitional role ensures and enhances employee engagement.

The last but definitely not the least, transformational role of the HR manager transforms an employee into a partner in the organization. He starts identifying his own salvation and self –actualization through his role he plays in course of his duty in the organization. It is indeed a profound role of the HR manager.

iii. Should these roles depend on the ranks of the professional? Elaborate.

Yes, indeed. As has been narrated in this case study, these roles depend upon ranks the HR professional holds or occupies during his career. The demands on the maturity levels of the HR functionary is different for these four T's. At the junior most level, the role is transactional, requiring the minimum demand on his maturity as the role is routine and regular and mostly well formulated. A HR officer can justifiably do this job.

Next comes the translational role which calls for a high level of communication skill. The HR functionary should be thorough with what to communicate, when to communicate and how to communicate. Any mis-communication may prove disastrous for the organization concerned. A HR manager is required for this job.

Transition is a lofty goal of the organization and has got strategic dimensions. Transitional methods can't be applied as a blanket measure for all the employees of a certain seniority and maturity. Indiscriminate transition is bound to fail. After effective translation, the management should be vigilant and watchful enough to identify which employees deserve the most to be transformed into a real asset for the organization and let them have the transition at the initiative of the company. It may involve a series of training and grooming the future pillars of strength for the company. They will serve as role models for others. This role demands a very high position and maturity which is available mostly at the GM level.

The last one i.e. the transformational role is fit to be an exclusive reserve for the member of the Board of Directors. Simply because, he may, after transforming himself, have to transform executives up to the GM level and be a role model for them. The truth is that a few Directors can step into this role and fulfil it satisfactorily. Certain evolved professionals at GM level, though exceptional, may be able to render justice to this role.

iv. Does any of these four T, s have anything to do with strategic HRM? Elaborate.

Yes, as has been explained in the answer to the previous question, touch of strategy can be traced from the level of translation itself. The interpretation of the ramifications of the management policies for the different classes and cadres of employees will depend on strategy. This strategic content increases Subsequently for transition and transformational roles.

The entire human resources base of the organization would be classified into categories and preferential treatment would be accorded to the class which is considered strategically important. Thus, human resources management can be used as a strategic weapon in the hands of the management to beat the competitor or acquire a higher market share.

FIRST TIME MANAGERS AND DELEGATION BLUES

It is widely known and acknowledged in the theory of management that in an organizational pyramid, there are three stages universally, quite independent of the organization's respective area of activity. This is comprehensively or commonly applicable regardless of whether the organization is product or service based or whether it is a brick and mortar or knowledge based. These three stages are, from bottom to top, operating, business/tactical and strategic or top levels. It is rather interesting to note how an executive, when promoted to the next higher stage i.e. business/tactical stage from the lowest i.e. the operational stage due to seniority, fails to perform owing to the lack of the requisite competence demanded in the new stage.

For a classic example, take the case of our Sampath Kumar, the blue –eyed boy of his immediate boss. Sampath Kumar's immediate boss was instrumental in getting him promoted because the boss was very happy with him. That was not the case with the boss's other sub-ordinates i.e. Sampath's peers. Sampath was exceptionally loyal and obedient to his immediate boss. Sampath used to interpret his relationship with the boss more as one of servitude than partnership. He did not consider his boss as a critical source of support. He used to fear him of being vulnerable in his presence. He did not want the boss to know his weaknesses lest his boss thought that he made a mistake in promoting him. He used to cover up all his failing assignment until he got them back in control. He used to wait for the boss to initiate meetings and ask for the reports. The boss initially liked this restraint, but it put tremendous pressure on him to keep communicating with Sampath.

When Sampath was promoted, he was told point blank, by the higher ups that so far his performance was above average as an individual performer, but, henceforth, he would not be working alone; he would lead a team and get things done. His performance would be measured by the performance of the whole team. He would have to command and motivate the team and the cracks in his competence started showing up. He was given big responsibilities with tight deadlines. His team came under tremendous pressure to produce results. Sampath did not learn how to delegate and tried to do everything himself. He believed that he could do any job better than his team mates. He also feared that if he assigned prestigious projects to his team mates, they would grab all the credits and recognition and visibility of his own contribution would be compromised. He also believed that he could add value only by doing the tasks himself and was not sure whether his other team members would do adequate justice to the task i.e. to his satisfaction.

These shortcomings on his part were too visible to his superiors and they took a serious cognizance of this issue. Quite rightly, they decided to send Sampath for advanced management training for middle managers in one of the prestigious institutes conducting the same. Sampath felt quit rejuvenated and came to terms with the idea of delegation. The management spent quite a good amount for the training and expected it to be a panacea for all of Sampath's shortcomings. But that was not to be. When he came back and commenced delegation, i.e. giving important assignments to his immediate sub-ordinates, he was supervising them so closely that they felt uncomfortable as if their accountability was not there. They also retaliated by non-cooperation i.e. refusing to take responsibility. Their fear was that they would be made convenient scape goats i.e. discredit for any failure would be dumped on their heads whereas the credit for any success would be grabbed by Sampath Kumar.

Now, the management was left wondering as to what to do with Sampath Kumar as the performance of his team did not improve. They were seriously contemplating asking him to leave.

Questions:

i. Who was at the wrong side, Sampath Kumar or his immediate boss or the higher ups? Explain.

Of course, when the deficiency was with Sampath Kumar, he can't be absolved of all the blames, he has to share his part in the problem but definitely he was not the main culprit. The lion's share of the blame should go his immediate boss. The lack of self-confidence with the spirit of servitude that Sampath Kumar was displaying at the operating level was very pleasing to his immediate boss's ego, so he did not bother to correct him. Sampath Kumar never asserted himself and his boss felt very safe and in the bargain, did not develop Sampath Kumar which was his bounden duty as the immediate superior. Neither the top management can be exonerated; it was incumbent upon them also to observe these deficiencies in Sampath Kumar and advice his immediate boss accordingly.

ii. What is delegation? What is its importance in management? Is it essential for management?

Delegation is one of the most important management exercises. It is empowering the junior with more and more authority of the senior. By virtue of this exercise, i.e. delegation, a junior is authorized to act on behalf of the senior sharing his power and authority. It should be noted and remembered that only authority can be delegated, not responsibility. In the theories of management, whenever a junior is empowered to act using the powers of his superior, the responsibility for the consequences of the action always lies with the senior who has delegated his powers. In other words, just because a senior has bestowed his power and authority to his sub-ordinate to act on his behalf, he can't escape the consequences of the action of the sub-ordinate. The senior's responsibility and accountability remains unaltered and intact.

Delegation is an extremely important management action by which a senior develops and grooms his subordinate who shares the authority but not the responsibility, so, as such, he is free to act without the Damocles sword of accountability and responsibility hanging precariously on his head. It is the responsibility that the junior dreads the most. He should be empowered to act fearlessly.

Yes, the act of delegation is essential in management and without this capacity, a senior is not much worth his salt.

iii. What are the merits and demerits of delegation?

It has already been stated in the answers to the previous questions that delegation is a necessary management exercise by which a sub-ordinate is built up to take over the senior's position in the hierarchy when the senior moves up the ladder or departs due to resignation, retirement or any other reason for separation. By virtue of this management exercise, a worthy sub-ordinate gets charged up or enthused as he is given an opportunity to act in a position bigger than his shoes i.e. higher than his position in the ranks. Through delegation, a subordinate is bestowed with authority not just commensurate but higher than his existing responsibility and he gets encouraged to act big and may even enjoy the feeling of occupying a higher position before actually being in that position. So, delegation clearly serves as a tool for motivation. This is for the subordinate.

For the senior who delegates, the exercise is no less beneficial. If a senior believes that a particular individual or even a group of his subordinates is capable of handling, at least, a part of his jobs, he gets relieved of the easier part of his job and can concentrate more on the more challenging and difficult part. So, by delegating, he effectively improved his own effectiveness. In management, a senior's astuteness is judged by the finesse and dexterity with which he delegates and trims down his work.

But, for disadvantages, delegation is a tricky and risky exercise, in some senses, for both the junior and the senior. For an uninspired, unambitious and unprepared junior, delegation of higher authority may seem burdensome and overwhelming, which he is asked to undertake over and above his existing work load. For such subordinates, it may seem penal and demotivating. There is one more factor adding to his discomfiture. He may think that everything will be done by him using powers beyond him but the credit for its success will be grabbed by the boss.

For the senior also the exercise is not that simple and straight forward. He has to be very judicious in selecting the subordinate to whom he can delegate a part of his authority. Simply because, it can be misused, if fallen in the wrong hands and he would be held responsible for lack of discretion and foresight. There are more dimensions to his challenge. An over smart subordinate, when given higher powers, may even usurp the authority of his superior and make him appear redundant in eyes of the higher ups and he would lose his power forever

iv. What is the difference between decentralization and delegation?

Decentralization is an exercise in designing an organizational structure. We get a decentralized structure when more number of people at lower levels is empowered to take more and more important decisions. Decentralization results in independence of making decisions and taking the necessary corresponding actions at comparatively lower levels.

Now, if we have a careful second look at the definition of delegation given earlier, we may easily conclude that the two terms are closely linked with each other and their relationship is such that delegation is the means and decentralization is the end. In other words, we obtain a decentralized organization structure by means of delegation.

v. What are the lessons in OB and HR you learn from this case study?

For an astute and eager learner, there are quite a few important lessons that can be learned:

a. In a hierarchical organization structure, a senior officer should take meticulous care in developing his subordinates to take higher and higher responsibility and using higher and higher authority. It is a relentless exercise.

b. When a senior indulges in feeling unwarrantedly pleased by an undue display of servitude and obedience by his immediate subordinate, he should note that he is failing in his duty in developing the subordinate.

c. According to William Edward Deming, the world renowned stalwart in Total Quality Management, any malady in an organization can be traceable to the top i.e, the accountability for the malady starts from the top. This case is also no exception. When an officer in the middle level fails to notice shortcomings in his subordinates and hence, fails to develop him, a malady is said to have set in and that should not escape the attention of the top management. Timely measures should be taken to correct it.

d. When an executive in the operating level is promoted to the next business level as per seniority, he may not be able to catch up with his new role readily and may require help. Sending him for advanced management training is a generalized morale boosting approach, though very costly, may not be very effective with officers having specific problems as in this case. Personal counseling by external organizational experts could be an effective measure.

e. Executives at the operating levels should be sent for training in leadership grooming and personality development periodically and regularly. These executives should be made to feel that the organization cares for their growth. The art of effective delegation has to be a necessary part of such training.

CASE STUDY 37

MANAGING ABOVE AVERAGE AND GENIUSES – A FEW CHALLENGES

The scenario: Gemini Electronics Ltd.   **Time: late seventies**

Dr. G.V. Rao, the General Manager of Gemini Electronics was a resolute person in the true sense of the term. In those days, Gemini Electronics, a mid-size electronic industry in the public sector under the Ministry of Defense, used to have only one GM in-charge of the whole factory. Dr. Rao was exceptional at least in one sense. He was one of those rarest professionals who migrated from academics to industry, instead of the other way round. He, a product of Benares Hindu University (BHU) in Electrical Engineering, was a believer in the dictum that strong engineering professionals can be built up in reputed institutions and not industries. He had tremendous fascination for reputed institutions i.e. once an engineer is from an average institution, the industry where he is working can't do much for his caliber; he remains an average for life. This blind faith in the excellence of the institutions seemed to have sinister implications as the turn of events proved later. He migrated from academics to industry as the Chief of R & D in Gemini Electronics and became the GM by virtue of seniority as DGM.

Once he was at the helm of affairs, he was bent upon taking measures in tune with his conviction and wanted to bring about revolutionary changes in the company's recruitment policies. In those days, campus recruitment was not in vogue; industry was dominated by public sector and recruitment used to be by open advertisements in the news papers followed by entrance test, short listing and personal interview at the company's premises. The selection was not any institution specific and a graduate engineer had to join as an 'engineering probationer' for one year, upon successful completion of which the probationer would be absorbed in the regular cadre as an Assistant Engineer. There was no discrimination based on whether the applicant was an engineering graduate or a post graduate degree holder or in which institute he had studied. All were treated on par for appointment as well as for further career advancement.

Dr. Rao, during his initial years in the industry, observed that there were a very few graduate engineers from premium institutions and post graduate engineers from any institution for that matter, joining Gemini Electronics as probationers. "It is only due to lack or absence of any incentive, whatsoever." – He thought. The reason for the small number of trainees from the premium institutions and PG degree holders, however handful were there, was that most of them hailed from Bangalore city itself or the nearby areas. They wished to get employment in their home town which acted as an incentive. "The whole industry is remaining a mediocre one because of this policy." – Dr. Rao concluded. AS a GM in-charge of the factory, he prevailed upon the BOD to bring about a change in the HR policy. He, along with the Head, R & D, decided to visit the campuses of all the five IITs those days, BHU, Roorkee and two RECs (NITs now) at Trichy and Surathkal. Premium institution graduates would be given two advance increments i.e. two years' seniority while joining and their training period would be waived off (that made virtually three years' seniority) and the PGs would be absorbed at one rank higher to start with – he decided.

The moment this new HR policy was announced and circulated in writing, all hell broke loose. All the existing assistant engineers were agitated and launched loud protests: "That means, freshers are coming as bosses from the day one and we are all fools of the first order. Three years of service in the industry has gone down the drain, added no value." – They contended. A few of them got an appointment fixed and met Dr. Rao, representing the whole community of assistant engineers in the factory, expressed their grievances and a sense of injustice done to them by the management. "The problem with you, i.e. the existing assistant engineers is that you were born three years too early and studied in the run of the mill institutions and that is not exactly my fault." – Dr. Rao said and packed them off.

Dr. Rao carried out his resolution, regardless. Twenty graduates and ten post graduates from the premier institutions joined and were directly posted in various departments without any induction training. All the PGs were posted in only the R & D departments. But, by all means, they were an isolated lot. They were treated as intruders from outside and nobody co-operated with them. They found it hard to gel with the others and were made to feel like fish out of water. The new comers' attitude and behavior also contributed handsomely to the mal-adjustment. They wanted to do things in their own way. They knew that they were the best in their craft and they believed that none could give them any useful suggestion and feedback. They considered themselves as a class of their own and wished to be left alone to manage their craft. They also found the work in Gemini Electronics monotonous and unchallenging. After a few months, they started leaving as there was no training there was no service bond either. Nobody could stop them. On the other hand, the morale of the existing assistant engineers was also very low and that adversely affected the company's performance.

Dr. Rao realized that somewhere he had gone wrong.

Questions:

i.   Do you also subscribe to Dr. Rao's conviction that engineers are made in institutes and not industry?

Well not exactly. Engineering institutes, however renowned, expose a student to the theoretical concepts. But, engineering is not only all about theories. The environment and scope in institutions are too restricted and confined to give a student adequate practical exposure for him to become a good engineer. In fact, it is a judicious mixture of theoretical concepts and practical exposure that make an engineer.

So, even if an individual is not from a so called renowned engineering college, but is keen and eager to learn the nuances of engineering, he can become a great engineer provided he works in a good engineering industry. On the other hand, a brilliant brat from a renowned institution, who is too proud of his upbringing and pedigree, may not make a good engineer.

In fine, an educational background from a renowned institution definitely helps, but is not the final word in the world of profession.

ii. Do you think Dr. Rao's academic background could contribute to such a conviction?

Yes, at least to some extent. That is the most unfortunate misconception among the professionals in India, be it in the fields of engineering, medicine or even law. There is a healthy mutual disregard and disrespect between the academic institutions and the corporates and hence, in our country, they can rarely come together and contribute to the profession and thereby enrich it. Sometimes this mutual lack of confidence acquires tragic proportions.

iii. Was the change in HR policy brought about by the company right for the company?

The decision to bring about drastic changes in HR policy had its own problems, but overall, it was good for the long term interest of the company. That way Dr. Rao's vision was correct. He was genuinely keen to have the company's performance improved by bringing in more intelligent and gifted people from renowned institutes. The move could improve the company's image also. The fact that the policy failed to bring about the desired result was not because of Dr. Rao's shortsightedness or lack of wisdom. It is a classic case of failure of the HR professionals in the company who should have advised Rao how to implement the policy. The real issue was not the policy per se, but its faulty implementation.

iv. What measures the company should have taken to make the policy work?

Dr. Rao should have been advised to take the following measures so as to increase the chances of success of his policy:

a. Before the policy was announced which struck the existing assistant engineers as a bolt from the blue, Dr. Rao should have called all of them for a meeting and discuss/explain the merits of the policy, its long term benefits and reasons for its implementation. He should have also asked for constructive suggestions as to how to protect the interests of the affected assistant engineers.

b. The recruitment interview which was held in the campuses should have been conducted as a preliminary screening interview to select students who would be eligible to appear at a tough written test followed by a final interview to be conducted at the company's premises. He should have allowed the existing assistant engineers also to appear and qualify them by the same process.

c. The company should have revamped its HR policy for recruitment, promotion and career development. Dr. Rao should have introduced a fast track career path together with the existing general track. Only so called brilliant engineers by virtue of his prestigious institutional background or service in the company who qualify in the tough test followed by an interview, would be admitted to that first track career.

d. The company should break the ego barrier, get in touch and come to understanding with the IITs to set a tough question paper for the entrance test which can be cleared by only engineers of far above average merit.

e. Before introducing the fast track career, the company should identify challenging jobs that require merit above average and redesign them to suit the meritorious and innovative engineers.

f. There should be extensive training programs for executives in the general track cadre to opt and qualify for the fast track cadre, so that the aspirants can appear in the test and qualify.

v. What lessons in HR and OB you learn from this case study?

Whatever remedial measures have been discussed in the answer to the previous question, all belong to the HR and OB domain only. However, the following lessons also can be taken for consideration:

a. Any phenomenal improvement in the performance of the organization takes time and has to be brought about very cautiously and patiently. Any drastic measure, however merited, will mostly backfire and prove counterproductive.

b. Improvement in the performance of the organization can't be done by ignoring the interests of the existing people.

c. Fresh blood from outside should not be imposed on the existing staff without induction training. Induction training is more about behavioral rather than technical aspects. It is also about cultural adjustment. It should not be bypassed as a matter of policy.

d.   Brilliant and above average people will not be able to do justice to mundane jobs. They will look for jobs which have appeals to their brilliance and above average caliber.

e.   Brilliant professionals are, in general, more dedicated to their profession rather than to any specific organization. They seek professional challenges wherever they go. That should be provided for them to stick around.

f.   Nobody, however brilliant, can function effectively in a hostile and unwelcome atmosphere. Conducive environment and atmosphere will have to be created before bringing in fresh talents.

g.   Existing people should be taken care of first before bringing in fresh talents. They should not be made to feel left to their fate and uncared for.

CASE STUDY 38

TATA MOTORS DOES AWAY WITH DESIGNATIONS

(The Economic Times-Wealth: June 12–18, 2017)

Tata Motors, India's largest automobile company by revenue, has decided to scrap designations and create a fatter organization as it looks to establish an environment in which team work inspired creativity can flourish. Designations such as General Manager, Senior General manager, Deputy General Manager, Vice-president and Senior Vice-President are among those that would be consigned to the scrap heap.

The company told employees that the move will create "a mind-set free of designations and hierarchy." About 10,000 employees of Tata Motors will be affected by this move – a senior executive said. All the managers with a team reporting to them will simply have the job title of "Head' followed by the function or department after their names. Employees who are individual contributors are largely at the front ends and do not have any team member reporting to them, will just use the function or department after their names.

The Human Resources recast, among the most sweeping in corporate India in recent times, will lead to a flattening of hierarchy levels to just five from fourteen. "More roles have moved than people, people need to grow in terms of breadth and depth. We need to break the slice across the functions."-said Gajendra S. Chandel, Chief Human Resources Officer at Tata Motors.

The company expects that the move will help Tata Motors put in place a work culture that is in line with those at global companies. The move will enable the company to move away from routine promotions that an employee gets purely by virtue of the time spent in the harness.

"In a competitive market such as ours, we are focused on empowering our employees and enabling optimal productivity which we believe, is possible with a reduced line of reporting, making the performance tracking process simple and transparent." – The spokesman added.

The "Organizational Effectiveness" (OE) program has been one of the core initiatives under the company's transformational journey, and to enable this, a detailed study of how to improve the speed, simplicity and agility within the company was conducted.

"With the support of an external agency, the details of the new structure have now been finalized and are being implemented." – The spokesperson said.

"This exercise, coupled with our other strategic initiatives as part of the company's transformational journey will enable Tata Motors to achieve global mind-set, through a strong and continued focus on operational excellence and robust processes." – The spokesperson further added.

The auto major has already reduced its managerial workforce by up to 1500 people domestically as part of the organizational restructuring exercise.

Questions:

    i.   Why hierarchies are need to be incorporated in an organizational design? Hierarchies are inherent in the definition of an organization itself. An organization is a collection of people who have come together for a common purpose and have a hierarchy among themselves. A group of people who have come together for a common purpose does not make an organization. A hierarchy or ranking of some sort is a must. Ranking provides a chain of command as a superior rank has the power to command over the subordinate rank. Each and every position in the organizational hierarchy has a well-defined authority and responsibility. A holder of a lower position in the organization has to abide by the direction or command or order of his senior otherwise there will be chaos and disorder and nothing can be accomplished. Such a collection of people will defeat its own purpose.

ii. Why the number of ranks in the hierarchy of a conventional brick and mortar organization is usually more than that of knowledge based organization?

Yes, in general, it is true that the number of ranks is more in a brick and mortar organization compared to knowledge based organization. That is because the manner and pattern of wealth creation in these two types of organizations are different. In conventional brick and mortar organizations, products and service are made or rendered by virtue of the infrastructure and man-machine interaction by the blue collar workers. White collar workers do not participate or contribute directly to production. So, strict monitoring and supervision is required. To implement that, we need a multilayered command structure.

Whereas, in the knowledge based counterpart, products are made or services are rendered by the white collar workers themselves and the roles of blue collars are marginal and meager. So, strict supervisions and disciplining are normally not called for. Hence, knowledge based organizations have, traditionally, a much flatter organization structure.

Moreover, as an extension of the same line of reasoning, in brick and mortar companies, we generally need a supervisory cadre intervening between the blue collar and managerial cadre for better co-ordination; that is not the case for knowledge workers who are managers themselves. Supervisory cadre adds to the number of ranks.

iii. What is your judgment and line of thinking regarding the efficacy of this bold and exceptional move by Tata Motors? Is the optimism expressed by the spokespersons regarding the move justified?

Tata Motors is, by all means, a brick and mortar company and definitely its move to abolish hierarchies in its organization structure, as per the advice of an external OD intervention specialist, is a bold one. The gamut of operation of the company can be broadly classified into two distinct classes. One is manufacturing passenger cars and commercial trucks and the other is sales and distribution of the same. Obviously, this proposed organization structure without ranks or drastically reduced ranks will be more effective in the service areas rather than the core manufacturing areas of activity. From the narration of the case it appears that the targeted area is of service. The narration is more silent about the manufacturing areas. Of course, it is a fact that a flatter organization design is now more in vogue as a practice worldwide. Tata Motors is only following that practice. The principal rationale behind this move is broadening the functional areas of executives and reducing the frequency of promotions. Once an executive is given a mouthful designation, he tends to get addicted to that and tries to create a comfort zone around the function indicated in the designation and starts believing that he is a master of that area only as the idea has been endorsed by the management. This narrowing of his field of activity hampers his functional diversity and versatility.

As far as the rationale behind reducing the frequency of promotion is concerned, it has been observed that promotions are more frequent in the career span when the ranks in the hierarchy are many. It is then evident that when the number of ranks is drastically reduced, the time gap between two consecutive promotions also would be larger. This has got certain beneficial effects.

When promotions are too frequent and nearby, the whole attention of the executive is diverted to his concern for promotion rather than his immediate duty at hand. He tries to please and impress his boss unduly by displaying his personality traits other than hard work, as hard work takes time to get favourably noticed. In the bargain, his core contribution suffers.

So, we can't rule out the optimism expressed by the company's spokesperson, ab – initio.

iv. What can be the potential pitfalls of this measure?

Particularly in Indian context, the potential pitfalls of this drastic and innovative measure are grave. An international research study on functioning of Indian corporate organizations reveals that we Indians are blind worshipers of authority. We, culturally, never tend to question authority and surrender unconditionally. This formal and positional authority is reflected in the designation given. When such designations themselves are abolished, this sense and smell of authority would be missing, however senior and knowledgeable the executive concerned is. So, in the absence of any fear of positional authority, the subordinates of a senior will be likely to take him for granted and this disregard has potential to create chaos and disorder. In the bargain, this will hamper the organization's progress. There is one more adverse fall out of making promotions few and far between. If a promotion appears too far in the time horizon, it would always seem too early to put up hard work and incumbents will tend to think that any hard word put in long before promotion will be forgotten while promotion consideration is made. Infrequent promotions may also have a demotivating effect.

So, as prerequisite for the success of this move, a cultural transformation and shake up is called for.

v. Why did Tata Motors need an external agent for its own organization development and re-design?

Organization development and redesign is a highly specialized professional management job and chances are high that the internal functionaries in the HR and OB areas may not have the requisite expertise or may not be equipped to do. The main reason for the same is that, for a particular organization, such exercises are undertaken very infrequently, if ever, and irregularly. On the other hand, for an external OD intervention expert who has many corporate clients, he may have to undertake such professional exercise for one client or the other regularly and he gains the requisite experience.

Hence, though costly, hiring an external OD intervention expert makes a lot of sense.

vi. Analyze the implications of this managerial initiative taken by Tata Motors from HR and OB angles.

In fact, to be precise, this entire exercise to bring about OD at the end, adopting removal of designations as a means, happens to be in the realm of HR and OB, particularly OB. The managerial implications of this intervention are profound:

a. To start with, there may be utter confusion and chaos when the hitherto visible conventional and time tested chain of command becomes obscured. Folks in the ranks will get confused as to whom to report, from whom to take command, whom to give orders, from whom to take advice and instructions etc. It will take some time for the dust to settle down.

b. In the absence of the conventional and defined lines of command, performance evaluation norms and criteria may have to be reworked. Somewhere along the way, the clear cut demarcation between efforts and results may get obscured. Someone may receive undue credit for someone else's effort or alternatively get punished for someone else's lapses or mistakes. This eventuality may demand extraordinary caution and vigil on the part of the HR and OB functionaries for quite some time to come.

c. Folks in the ranks may need training to cope up with the altered situation and who would impart this professional training will turn out to be an important decision, whether it would be done by the internal functionaries or the external experts hired for the OD intervention. The issue has got both behavioral and cost implications.

d. The senior executives who were, so far, basking in the glory of their hard earned position with mouthful designations may feel let down and betrayed. They may opt for a premature departure by voluntarily retiring. This move on their part will have tremendous HR, OB and financial implications. Sudden vacuum at the top of the tactical level will have to be filled up at the earliest. The new incumbent, after getting sudden and unexpected promotion, is likely to be under euphoria and may take time to adjust behaviorally at the new position and responsibility; his effectiveness will have to be compromised for some time.

e. Such unexpected bonanza to one incumbent will upset many others and their effectiveness also will have to be compromised.

f. Such cumulative and cascading effects will take its toll on the Profit and Loss Account, at least, for the current year and the Board of Directors will have a tough time to convince the shareholders in the forthcoming AGM.

www.ingramcontent.com/pod-product-compliance
Lightning Source LLC
Chambersburg PA
CBHW031809190326
41518CB00006B/257